EXIT
BERLIN

EXIT
BERLIN

———

How One Woman
Saved Her Family
from Nazi Germany

Charlotte R. Bonelli

With translations from the German by

Natascha Bodemann

Yale UNIVERSITY PRESS
New Haven & London

———

Published with assistance from the foundation established in memory of
Philip Hamilton McMillan of the Class of 1894, Yale College.

Yale University Press books may be purchased in quantity for educational, business,
or promotional use. For information, please e-mail sales.press@yale.edu (US office) or
sales@yaleup.co.uk (UK office).

Designed by Lindsey Voskowsky.
Set in Bodoni and Adobe Caslon type by Integrated Publishing Solutions.
Printed in the United States of America.

Library of Congress Cataloging-in-Publication Data

Bonelli, Charlotte, 1956–
    Exit Berlin : how one woman saved her family from Nazi Germany / Charlotte
Bonelli ; with translations from the German by Natascha Bodemann.
      pages cm
    Includes bibliographical references and index.
    ISBN 978-0-300-19752-5 (hardback)
      1. Hatch, Luzie—Family—Correspondence. 2. Hatch, Arnold—Correspondence.
3. Jews—Germany—Correspondence. 4. Jews—United States—Correspondence.
5. Holocaust, Jewish (1939–1945)—Personal narratives. 6. World War, 1939–1945—
Jews—Germany. I. Bodemann, Natascha, translator. II. Title.
    DS134.4.B66 2014
    940.53'180922—dc23
    [B]   2013041647

A catalogue record for this book is available from the British Library.

This paper meets the requirements of ANSI/NISO Z39.48–1992
(Permanence of Paper).

10 9 8 7 6 5 4 3 2 1

For my three aunts of blessed memory, Carmela Bonelli, Beatrice Spector, and Ida Spector, each a unique treasure. If I had only had one such aunt, I could have said *Dayenu*. That I had three was surely a blessing from the Good Lord.

CONTENTS

PART TWO
December 1938–August 1939

PART THREE
September 1939–October 1941

Illustrations follow page 204

ACKNOWLEDGMENTS

Long ago, when I was a graduate student applying for an independent project, my adviser warned me, with a sharply pointed finger, "Writing is a solitary process." In terms of *Exit Berlin*, she was only partially correct. Researching and writing the book did include innumerable solitary hours, but the book also introduced me to an array of warm and wonderful people. This was an unexpected joy of *Exit Berlin*. I am pleased to be able to thank all of those who contributed.

Often people don't realize the historic value of items, tossing them into the trash, where they are forever lost. Fortunately, this was not the case when Attorney Roger Blane discovered Luzie Hatch's correspondence. He was determined to save the collection and bring it to the public. It was Roger who called me to discuss donating the correspondence to the American Jewish Committee Archives. In expressing my thanks to him, I speak not only for myself but for the entire AJC family. I would also like to thank Attorney Steve Solomon, Luzie's estate executor, for his interest and cooperation in this project. *Exit Berlin* would not have been possible without their support.

Ralph Hatch, Luzie Hatch's half-brother, supplied documents, photos, and very valuable memories. He opened his home to me on many occasions, each visit being not only productive but enjoyable thanks to his wonderful sense of humor and hospitality. Pat Roth, Arnold Hatch's granddaughter, and Gloria Hatch, his daughter-in-law, are also to be thanked for their cooperation. As probably is always the case, this project turned out to be lengthier than anticipated. Still, Pat's interest in the project never wavered.

Inge Friedlander, Hilde Übelacker, Fred Kirschner, and Eva Emmerich all granted me interviews, recalling their World War II experiences. These interviews were not always easy, for they called forth extraordinarily painful memories, in some instances, experiences that until our meeting had been completely locked away. I greatly appreciate their efforts. The stories they told and the information they supplied added a new dimension to this book. I also communicated with a number of people via email or phone. All were cooperative and instrumental in putting me on the right research path. Rose Feldman, webmaster of the Israel Genealogical Society; Michael Merose and Dan Mendels, two of Luzie Hatch's descendants; the late Henry Rodwell, a former L. S. Mayer employee; and Michael Chaut are all due huge thanks. Ilse Ohlms kindly volunteered to work with the letters written in old German script, rewriting them in modern script and thereby saving Natascha Bodemann, the translator, both time and angst.

Visits to the Landesarchiv in Berlin and the Stadtmuseum/-archiv in Baden-Baden were extremely productive. I am truly indebted to Dagmar Rumpf, of the Baden Archiv, who put me in contact with Hilde Übelacker, a Camp Gurs survivor, and Angelika Schindler, a historian of Baden's Jewish community. Not only did Angelika fill in important details about Jewish life in Baden, but she led me to another Gurs survivor, Fred Kirschner. Here in the United States, the Spindle Historical Society provided images of Arnold Hatch's factory. I researched the American roots of Luzie's family at Congregation Beth Emeth, in Albany, New York. What a pleasure it was to see how the synagogue has preserved its history. In addition, I would like to note how warmly I was received by the Beth Emeth's archivists, Adelaide Muhlfelder and Patricia Snyder. Lisa Adele Miller, a dear college friend of mine, generously pitched in on some of the Albany-related research. Misha Mitsel and Sherry Hyman of the American Joint Distribution Committee Archives, in typical fashion, went out of their way to be helpful.

At times, despite exhaustive research, I was still left with unanswered questions about elements of this period in history. I thank Richard Evans of Cambridge University and Marion Kaplan of New York University for taking the time to answer my queries.

Many people from the American Jewish Committee, past and present, deserve thanks for their help: Roselyn Bell, Ephraim Gabbai, Shifra Sharbat, Mirja Muller, Larry Grossman, and Lena Altman. My dedicated assistants, Cuc Huong Do and Desiree Guillermo, are deserving of special praise. With their characteristic positive demeanor and efficiency, they performed a seemingly endless list of tasks related to this book. Linda Krieg, AJC's director of graphic arts, was a constant source of encouragement, even in the face of some obstacles and inevitable delays. Marilyn Braverman, now retired from AJC, offered information on Luzie's work history. Gerri Rozanski, former director of AJC's regional offices, was the one person who had a close personal relationship with Luzie. With her information and stories, a more complete understanding of Luzie emerged. A special thanks to AJC Executive Director David Harris for his encouragement and interest in this project.

Lydia Freudenstein read early versions of the manuscript, offering many solid suggestions. Liora Brosh, a friend of many years and an outstanding English professor, convinced me that the letters could be framed in a narrative. I was skeptical but am glad that she persisted. My sister, Deborah Bonelli, brother, Jonathan, and mother, Esther, listened to endless conversations about this book. And it was my sister who changed the title from *Berlin Exit* to *Exit Berlin*.

Even as a young child, I always loved history books. This fondness for history was no doubt increased in Glastonbury High School, where I had the benefit of two outstanding history teachers, Katherine Stingle and Deborah Willard (then Skauen). At Skidmore College, I studied with the late professor Tad Kuroda. For good reason, he was a campus legend. As I researched and wrote this book, I often thought of the lessons he had taught me. I suppose this is the greatest tribute one can offer a former professor. Those of us who were his students were deeply saddened to learn of his passing in 2010.

Natascha Bodemann has been with me since the start of this work years ago. She began as a translator who brought more than her linguistic skills to this project. Natascha offered keen insights on the letters and as someone who had lived in Germany helped me plan my trips to Berlin. Even when the sailing was far from smooth, Natascha remained enthusiastic and optimistic.

There is little to say about my literary agent, Carol Mann, other than that she is exceptional. I am grateful to her for the effort she put into this project.

The last person on my long "thank you" list is Bonny V. Fetterman, a superb editor with valuable knowledge of the publishing industry. Bringing this manuscript to publication was not an easy task; I am indebted to Bonny for her wisdom, faith in this endeavor, and friendship. It is no exaggeration to say that there never would have been an *Exit Berlin* without Bonny V. Fetterman.

HECHT FAMILY TREE

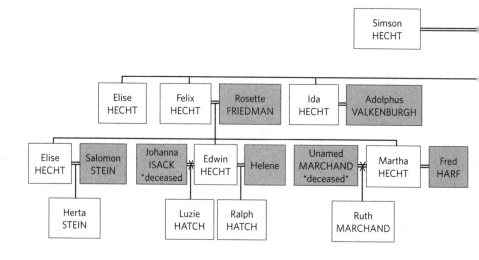

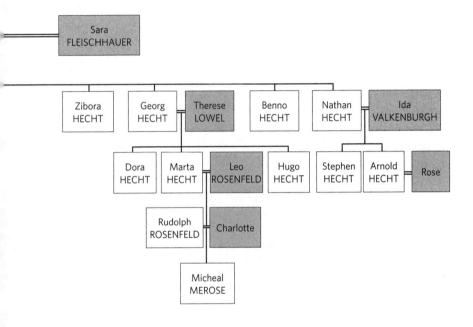

ISACK FAMILY TREE

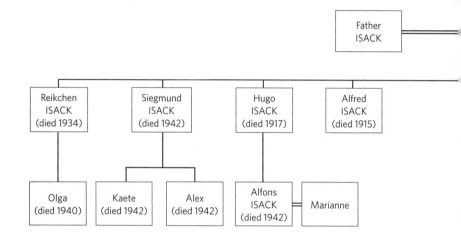

Father
ISACK

Reikchen
ISACK
(died 1934)

Siegmund
ISACK
(died 1942)

Hugo
ISACK
(died 1917)

Alfred
ISACK
(died 1915)

Olga
(died 1940)

Kaete
(died 1942)

Alex
(died 1942)

Alfons
ISACK
(died 1942)

Marianne

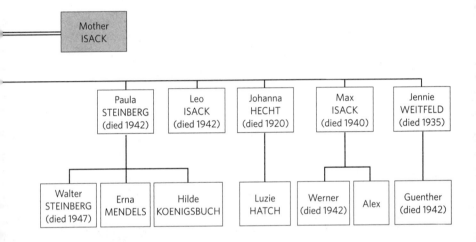

EXIT
BERLIN

HOW IT ALL BEGAN

Exit Berlin is based on a selection of letters from the American Jewish Committee's Luzie Hatch Collection. Luzie, a German Jew, fled to the United States from Germany in 1938. Four months after her arrival, she found employment in New York at the American Jewish Committee. Hired for a temporary position, she had a hunch, a correct one, that she might stay longer. Luzie worked at the AJC from 1939 until her retirement in 1977, and she was well known to everyone. Thus it was understandable that when these letters were discovered, after her death, by an estate executor, he called me, the director of the AJC Archives, and offered to donate her correspondence.

There is no shortage of letters written by German Jews who suffered through the Nazi period. Not only were German Jews dedicated letter writers, but they took care to save their work, and therefore we have an abundance of letters documenting the Jewish plight under the Nazis. Unlike other letter writers, however, Luzie frequently made copies of outgoing letters, later filing them with the incoming responses. She created a collection of matching correspondence. As Professor Henry Feingold, himself a refugee from Nazi Germany and an authority on the American response to the Holocaust, states, "We have hundreds of collections of letters from refugees, but what we have very little of . . . what is really rare, is something like this."

So what kind of historical record did Luzie Hatch leave behind? Not a diary, with just a single perspective, or a bundle of letters from one individual, but an unfolding story involving people in the United States, Germany, Vichy France, Bolivia, Shanghai, Palestine, and England. Because of the breadth of her correspondence, there is a broad range of WW II refugee history: information about US immigration law, the deportation of Jews from Baden and the Saarpfalz, Vichy internment camps, the Trans-Siberian escape route, Jewish refugees in Shanghai, and the Aryanization of Jewish businesses in Germany.

But the collection is more than just a historical document; it is also a personal family story. It is filled with the warmth, tension, appreciation, and misunderstandings that could exist in any family— but this family was dealing with the horrors of the Holocaust. We hear many voices in this correspondence, and the nuances, as well, are important to the story. Luzie serves not only as translator for her American cousin, Arnold Hatch, but as an intermediary advocating for her relatives in Germany and advising them how best to approach Arnold for help.

Luzie and her younger cousin Herta Stein left Berlin on November 16, 1938, just one week after the horrors of Kristallnacht. Disembarking in New York City with a photo as her guide, she searched the faces in the crowd for Arnold Hatch, her American-born cousin and rescuer. To her surprise, there was nothing distinctly German about Arnold or his brother Stephen. "They are real Americans," she wrote to her family in Berlin. "You do not notice that they have had a German father at all."

Once in America, Luzie would become the focal point for other Hecht family members trying to escape from Nazi Germany. Since Arnold Hatch did not know German, and his relatives in Germany knew little English, it was only natural that Luzie would take on her crucial role as intermediary. Yet it was not simply her linguistic skill that caused her German relatives to turn to her for assistance. From their viewpoint, the fact that Arnold had saved Luzie seemed to be evidence that she had been able to influence him. Could she not do the same for her aunts and cousins left behind in Germany? Thus, with Luzie as translator and go-between, an unending stream of requests from German relatives made their way to Arnold's desk, testing his financial strength, patience, and fortitude.

A crime of such enormity, the Holocaust remains vivid and poignant for American Jewry to this day. More than six decades later, the question of why the American Jewish community of Arnold Hatch's era didn't respond more forcefully to the needs of its European brethren still pulls at the American Jewish conscience.

Exit Berlin is a pathway back to the American Jewish setting of the 1930s and early 1940s. But the path does not lead to the world of commanding figures such as Rabbi Stephen Wise or Rabbi Abba Silver. It leads, instead, into the world of an "average" American Jew, a businessman in Albany, New York, an individual who had never thought he would be thrust into the politics of rescue. And it is here that *Exit Berlin* takes a new turn in Holocaust literature, giving us the second unique feature of Luzie Hatch's letters. Although much attention has been given to the records of religious and communal institutions, Jewish politicians, writers, and activists, little has been written about the response of individual Jewish American families to the tragic plight of their trapped relatives in Europe.

In 1933, after the death of his German-born father, Arnold Hatch assumed the presidency of Fuld & Hatch Knitting in Cohoes, New York. In addition to the responsibility of keeping the family business afloat during the Depression, a challenge in and of itself, Arnold had inherited the complex and ever-changing problem of responding to the needs of his German relatives with whom he had had little if any prior contact. The eighty-six letters written by Arnold Hatch over a seven-year period offer an intimate picture of how one Jewish American family faced not only the question of its moral obligations but the everyday realities of rescue.

Although he had the best intentions, Arnold found that he was unable to respond adequately to every request. In the most general sense, each relative had the same urgent need—emigration from Germany. However, their various ages, health conditions, financial statuses, and locations made each plea for assistance a new challenge.

Arnold's correspondence includes letters not only to relatives but to bank officials, shipping companies, the Hebrew Immigrant

Aid Society, the National Coordinating Committee for Aid to Refugees and Emigrants Coming from Germany, and US court and immigration officials. There was always a letter to write, and there were always nagging questions. Had his letter been received? Was a relative able to access the funds sent, or had a Nazi official pocketed the money? Had Arnold properly followed American immigration law?

In the 1920s, the United States had decided that it could no longer be so welcoming to the immigrant masses. Religious and racial nativism, along with popular fears that the foreign influx threatened the nation's economic security, resulted in the passage of restrictive immigration legislation. Yet the new quotas, established by Congress, proved to be only a first step. Those charged with enforcing the law were not without the power to further the cause of immigration restriction. From 1933 to 1945, the German quota of 25,957, which increased to 27,370 to represent both Germany and Austria following the Anschluss, rarely even approached the limit. In 1933, a mere 1,375 immigrants from Germany were admitted to the United States; in 1934, the figure was 3,556; and in 1935, German immigrants numbered 5,243.[1]

What motivated American consulate officials to be so stringent when reviewing applications? Most likely many factors worked in combination: anti-Semitism, antiforeign sentiment, fear that German spies could disguise themselves as refugees, economic concerns, and, in some cases, an overzealous bureaucratic personality. Whatever the reasons, the outcome, as historian Rafael Medoff writes, was that "for the entire period of the Nazi regime, 1933 to 1945, more than 190,000 quota spaces from Germany and Axis countries sat unused."[2]

The immigration law, the spread of war, and the ever-changing circumstances in Europe all combined to frustrate and, at times, exhaust Arnold Hatch. Despite his wealth, education, and social status, he was only one man standing against forces that were well beyond his control.

Arnold Hatch was separated from his German relatives not only by thousands of miles but by the additional chasm of differing perspectives that at times seemed even more impassable. The Depression was a major force in how this forty-five-year-old businessman viewed the world. He had seen families who had once inhabited his own comfortable business and social circles crushed by the economic collapse of 1929. Understandably, he wanted to plan, to be cautious, to know there would be employment and a means of support for those who arrived. But for those living under the increasingly brutal hand of Nazism, the first issue at hand was not one's economic future but the simple and vital need to escape, to be free, *to survive*.

Perhaps Arnold's caution would have been mitigated if he had fully comprehended the enormity of the evil enveloping Germany, but unfortunately, he never did. His failure to do so is obvious. For example, when his cousin Martha Marchand Harf wanted to take the Trans-Siberian rail route to Vladivostok, Arnold's response was that the plan was "insane." Yet, despite its risk and arduous nature, it seemed to Martha to be the only possible means of escape for her and her young daughter. Arnold urged Martha to be "rational" and to "stay in Cologne until this unfortunate war is over."

Luzie Hatch found herself sandwiched between these two profoundly conflicting forces: her American cousin's reasonable caution and the desperation of her relatives in Germany. It was a delicate situation for a single twenty-seven-year-old who was attempting to make her way in a new country.

This is the basic outline that emerged on my first reading of the collection. But I inevitably wanted to learn more about Luzie and those with whom she corresponded. Through the Internet, requests to the Yad Vashem Archives, newspaper advertisements, helpful tips from colleagues, and old-fashioned telephone book searches, I was able to track down some of the correspondents' relatives. They were always cooperative and contributed a rich supply of photographs, documents, and information.

My research task extended well beyond the discovery and collection of biographical material. A good deal of historical context was needed for the reader to navigate through the correspondence with ease and to enhance the educational value of Luzie's story. Thus there is information on a number of subjects including US immigration laws, conditions at the Vichy internment camps, refuge in Shanghai, and Aryanization of Jewish businesses in Germany.

Most letters selected for *Exit Berlin* have been shortened and at times edited. There was often a great deal of detail about immigration quotas and processes repeated time and time again. In order to write a compelling narrative, most of these elements have been removed. The same is true of references to relatives and friends who remained largely unknown or are tangential to the story. It must be stressed that the editing process was limited to punctuation, grammar, and minor deletions. The correspondent's words were not rewritten. I chose such limited editing in order to retain each writer's personality and perspective. The letters remain historical documents.

PART ONE

May 1933–
September 1938

1

Berlin Beginnings

It is ironic that Luzie Hatch came to this country, and left the world, on the heels of an evil wind. She fled Nazi Germany in 1938, one week after the Kristallnacht pogroms had torn through the Jewish community leaving 267 synagogues and 7,500 Jewish businesses burned to the ground or destroyed. Ninety-one Jews were murdered and nearly thirty thousand Jewish men were incarcerated. In her letters, Luzie referred to Kristallnacht as "the terrible days."

She died on September 16, 2001, just days after the 9/11 attacks, when terrorists had transformed an ordinary means of transportation, passenger planes, into weapons, killing thousands. On occasion, Luzie had taken visitors to see those two great World Trade Center Towers stretching skyward. In fact, in this book there is a photo of Luzie and her friends standing before the Towers. But after the attack there was just a gaping crater spewing an acrid smell that lingered for months. These events, Kristallnacht and September 11, were the bookends of her life in America.

When she sailed into the New York Harbor in November 1938, she thought she had left evil behind her. Luzie was young, only twenty-seven, but she was far from young when she passed away on September 16, 2001, at the age of eighty-nine. She had no children, and her estate executor, attorney Stephen Solomon, made the frequent visits to her bedside as her days diminished. They had known each other for decades.

Following Luzie's death, the task of dealing with her personal belongings fell to an associate of Stephen Solomon's, the attorney Roger Blane. While at her studio apartment, inventorying items to be sent to a Connecticut auction house—the usual possessions, furniture, books, and bric-a-brac—he stumbled on a collection of more than three hundred World War II era letters written by Luzie, her family members, her friends, and Berlin business colleagues. He insisted that I examine the collection.

Luzie Hatch, who had worked as an administrative assistant in a number of departments at the American Jewish Committee, retired long before I came to the AJC Archives, so I knew very little about her except for one important fact. She had spent a lifetime at AJC. How could I, the director of the archives, refuse to at least look at her letters? And so, on a brutally hot summer day, out of respect for her memory, I took the subway to Luzie's studio apartment in Forest Hills, New York.

Entering the apartment, I was immediately struck by the fact that it was "bursting" at the seams. How could it be otherwise? Luzie had lived in this studio apartment for sixty-one years. Every inch of the apartment was full. The bookshelves were packed so tightly that some books appeared to be popping out of the shelves. And she had put more than books on the shelves; they were amply dotted with tchotchkes: figurines of animals, children, and ceramic flowers.

It seemed as though Luzie Hatch had saved everything. There were maps and travel brochures from across the country, theater programs from decades ago, dozens of old medical and utility bills, and a 1975 Macy's department store receipt documenting the return of a sofa. The file cabinet drawers were so full and heavy that they seemed to resist my efforts when I first tried to pull them open.

The black and battered binder containing her years of correspondence was also tightly packed. Letters that had yellowed and grown brittle over the years protruded out beyond the binder's edge. They had probably been tucked away for decades before being pulled out of the cabinet drawer.

I had been skeptical of Roger Blane's enthusiasm for the letters. But that changed as I turned the pages and saw that Luzie had not only saved incoming letters but frequently made a copy of her outgoing letters. I realized I was holding a rare collection of matching correspondence. Turning to Roger, I told him that the AJC Archives would accept the collection. Pleased with my response, he left me to read the letters. In an effort to stave off the suffocating August heat, I tugged at the cord of the kitchen ceiling fan and was drawn into the Hatch family story.

"You can't imagine how this city devours you. You really barely have a moment to yourself. The distances in Berlin are not at all comparable to the ones here—and then we all have our heads too full and also have so much disappointing and sad correspondence to write that everything else takes a back seat." This was one of the first letters Luzie sent back to Germany after her arrival here in November 1938.

And there had been much correspondence to write. Week after week there were letters from her parents, aunts Paula Steinberg and Martha Marchand, cousins Alfons Isack and Dora Hecht, work colleagues, and others. But before introducing these relatives and friends, there is Luzie's immediate family, the Hechts of Berlin.

In many ways, the Hechts typified German Jewry. Like most German Jews, they made their home in an urban center. Luzie, her father, Edwin, stepmother, Helene, and half-brother Rolf, were part of the one-third of German Jewry who resided in Berlin.[1]

By chance, when visiting the city, I had booked a room in a district adjacent to the Hechts' Wilmersdorf neighborhood of West Berlin. Filled with the excitement of a first-time visitor, I had darted in and out of my modest pension a number of times before noticing a plaque indicating the building had been home to ORT's Berlin headquarters from 1937 to 1939.[2] Had Luzie and her family been among the hundreds of German Jews who had come to the ORT office desperate for a vocational training course that would provide them with a marketable skill in a new land? Perhaps, for my hotel was a short ten-minute walk to the Hecht residence.

While not wealthy, the Hechts were solidly middle class, if not upper middle class. Luzie's father had taken the typical career path for a German Jew. More than 50 percent of German Jews were employed in business or commerce, and so was Edwin Hecht. He worked as a merchandise manager at H. Joseph Company, a Jewish-owned department store. Like her father, Luzie also entered the business world. In January 1933, at age twenty-one, she secured a position as an assistant to a top executive at the prestigious firm of L. S. Mayer. At its founding in 1822, the company dealt in dry goods. By 1933, when Luzie joined the firm, its line had expanded and included leather goods, jewelry, and finery. With offices in Berlin, Frankfurt, Pforzheim, Paris, and New York, and with strong connections to L. S. Mayer Ltd. in London, the company sold its products to department stores, specialty stores, and wholesalers in North America, Europe, and the British colonies.

Henry Rodwell, a former employee of L. S. Mayer Ltd., recalls that the company was "a very well-considered and good employer in Germany and every Jewish father wanted his son to become an apprentice, if you like, with L. S. Mayer."[3] Edwin Hecht was probably delighted with his daughter's success. There is no doubt that the work suited Luzie's personality. She loved communicating with various customers, vendors, and offices in different parts of the world. When penning her reference letter an executive noted that "she was especially qualified to meet German and foreign customers hereby making use of her knowledge of the English and French languages."

Working at L. S. Mayer, Luzie was able to peek at the new trends in leather goods and jewelry before these items filled shop counters and windows in Berlin, Paris, and London. At times, Luzie did more than just assess the new merchandise. A former colleague wrote teasing her with a reminder of how Luzie used to take the new items and put on a little fashion show in the office. So her employment at L. S. Mayer was more than a paycheck, it was a passion.

Life at 12 Zähringerstasse, the Hecht residence, was typical for the time. Luzie's stepmother, Helene, was a housewife, busy with all the normal household chores and the task of watching over her very lively nine-year-old son, Ralph.

The family was not deeply religious. They did not eat only kosher meat, keep separate dishes for meat and dairy, or strictly observe the Sabbath. But neither were the Hechts totally cut off from their religious roots, and this was in large part due to Helene. "My mother was not a fanatic," recalls Ralph, "but she did have an identification."[4]

Although it was only on occasion that Helene walked to the neighborhood synagogue for Shabbat services, she made sure that the major Jewish holidays were always observed at the Hecht household.

"Highly assimilated" is the term often used to describe German Jews. Yet perhaps it is more accurate to speak of the Hechts as "highly acculturated." They did choose to live in Wilmersdorf, after all, a neighborhood with a significant Jewish presence; and their friends, as well as a large number of their coworkers, were mainly Jews.

Although Luzie lived in the same Wilmersdorf building as her father, stepmother, and brother, by the time she left Berlin in 1938, she had moved out and was renting a room from another family in the building. She was, of course, old enough to be independent, and her relationship with her stepmother, Helene, was rather strained. Johanna Hecht, Luzie's mother, had died when she was a child. Her father remarried when she was nine, an age where a warm relationship between child and stepparent might have been forged. But no such bond ever developed between Luzie and her stepmother. Ralph asserts that Luzie had always worshipped her mother and resented Helene's entrance into the family. He also recalls that when Luzie lay in hospice there was a large photo of her mother, along with a smaller one of her father, at the bedside.

This is the basic outline of Luzie's family, the Hechts of Berlin.

May 1933–September 1938
—

And the picture that emerges is of a family that was quite representative of Germany Jewry in terms of professions, home life, residence, and high degree of acculturation. They were certainly, in the 1920s and up to the rise of Hitler, quite at home in Germany.

After the war, after knowledge of the death camps was public, the horrifying photos printed, the individual nightmares told, people wondered, almost in disbelief, why German Jews hadn't recognized Hitler's threat from the start. Why didn't they leave earlier? How could they have stayed? Didn't they see what was happening?

When I broached this topic with Luzie's brother, Ralph, he leaned forward and bellowed, "Who could have thought they would put people in ovens? Who would have thought such a thing? My parents had been born there; my grandparents had been born there. My father fought in the German Army in World War I. And who the hell wants to leave their homeland?"[5] Ralph had answered my questions with force and sincerity, and no one can argue with the merit of his response. Yet there were additional reasons why so many were slow to recognize the Nazi danger.

When German president Hindenburg appointed Hitler chancellor of Germany on January 30, 1933, there had been no great panic among German Jews. They did not rush to foreign consulates for visas, start contacting relatives abroad, or make plans to sell their homes and businesses. Many believed that the responsibility of actually governing rather than simply rabble-rousing and performing at rallies, the presence of conservatives in the new government, and pressures from the outside world would somehow curb Nazi excesses.[6]

In fairness to German Jews, this assessment of Hitler's chancellorship was not limited to their community. With only two Nazis in Hitler's cabinet, it seemed reasonable to assume that his sphere of influence would be circumscribed. The makeup of the cabinet shows that Herr Hitler "had to accept significant restrictions." This was the opinion of the internationally well-known and liberal German newspaper, the *Frankfurter Zeitung*. Here in the United States *The New York Times* agreed: "The composition of the Cabinet leaves Herr Hitler no scope for the gratification of his dictatorial ambitions."[7]

Early on, this was how many assessed Hitler's future, but Luzie's father, Edwin, was decidedly not part of this majority. While so many around the Hecht family attempted to maintain what they thought was a sense of reason, not to fall victim to fear, Edwin Hecht, from the very outset, recognized the impending Nazi threat.

Hitler's ascent to power coincided with a sharp career reversal for Edwin Hecht, probably the first one of his life. It was at this time that a letter arrived at the Hecht household from the Karstatt Department Stores, Edwin's future employer, stating that due to "political circumstances" they were withdrawing their offer of a high-level executive position. The timing could not have been worse; he had already resigned from his position at a Jewish-owned Berlin department store. With no warning and through no fault of his own, he was suddenly out of work.

Yet Edwin Hecht was able to overcome this setback. He had a good personality, connections within the retail world, was well liked, and had wit, a mix of traits that allowed him to become self-employed, working as a sales representative for various German leather goods firms.

Every morning, he loaded his Opel with the sample merchandise that now filled the household, giving it the feel of a warehouse, and set off for sales visits to stores in Berlin and the outlying areas. The loss of his position with the Karstatt Department Stores was

May 1933–September 1938

18

unfortunate and unnerving, yet it did not ruin the family's well-being. Still, as Ralph would say, perhaps it was this experience which gave his father a "jolt, and made him see the handwriting on the wall from the very beginning."

In 1933, out of the total Jewish population of 525,000, roughly 37,000 Jews left Germany. Despite the strong reluctance of his wife, Helene, Edwin Hecht had wanted to be part of this initial emigration. With a mind of his own, it mattered little to him that his family and friends were not making plans to emigrate. But to leave their homeland, the Hechts would need to reconnect with Nathan Hatch, Luzie's great uncle, who had left Germany more than sixty years ago and lived more than four thousand miles away in Albany, New York.

2

From Hecht to Hatch

American Relations

According to family lore, Neuhaus, Bavaria, was simply too confining for Nathan Hecht. At the age of sixteen, he set sail for America on the *Westphalia,* arriving in New York City in June 1873. He had chosen a nation that was moving forward rapidly, expanding in all sectors: urban centers, agriculture, industry, and transportation. For someone who was unafraid of hard work and willing to take risks, with a creative spark and the blessing of good luck, opportunities were plentiful.

Little is known of Nathan's very early time in the United States. According to his obituary in the *Cohoes American,* he spent a short time in Schoharie County, near Albany, before settling in the state capital in 1878. The choice was a natural one, for Albany had a significant German Jewish population. Here he would find camaraderie with his compatriots, the advice of those already settled, and the possibility of finding a business partner. According to the Albany City Archives, in 1885, Nathan was working as a salesman at S. M. Valkenburgh and Company, a wholesale hosiery, furnishing goods, and notions establishment. One year later, according to the marriage records of Temple Beth Emeth, Albany's prominent German Reform congregation, Nathan, now twenty-four years old, married his employer's daughter, Ida Rose Valkenburgh. Although of German descent, Ida was not an immigrant but an Albany native. By the time of his marriage, Nathan had already anglicized his last name, changing it from Hecht to Hatch.

Eight years later, Nathan's sister Ida would also become part of the Valkenburgh family, marrying his brother-in-law, Adolphus Valkenburgh. Both marriages likely carried financial and social benefits for the young immigrants.[1]

In 1892, Nathan began what would be a very profitable partnership with David Fuld. The two entrepreneurs started manufacturing knit goods in Albany. Within fifteen years, the Albany location could no longer accommodate the growing demand for their products, and a plant was erected in the nearby bustling industrial center of Cohoes, New York. Eventually, the entire business would be consolidated in Cohoes.

Their success continued. In 1914, Fuld and Hatch Knitting patented its one-button union suit. Full-page magazine advertisements touted the men's underwear as the top of the line: "It has only one button—one master button conveniently placed at the chest. It does the work of a whole useless row. No buttons to break or fall off, no buttonholes to get torn." Independent stores throughout the nation, along with two of the country's top retailers, Sears and Roebuck and Montgomery Ward, carried the Fuld and Hatch one-button suit.

If Luzie's great uncle Nathan had come to America with high aspirations, he had indeed met if not surpassed them. When it was at full capacity, Fuld and Hatch Knitting employed five hundred workers. Nathan's financial success allowed him to build a spacious classical revival house above Albany's Washington Park. The 1920 census shows that the family employed both a cook and a maid.

The *Cohoes American* noted that it was not simply success in the business world that had made Nathan Hatch a respected figure in Albany but also his numerous philanthropic activities. He was a member of Temple Beth Emeth, served on the board of the Albany Orphan Asylum, and was a major contributor to Albany's Hebrew Benevolent Society. Nathan had also been a vice chairman of the Committee of Fifty, organized to raise funds for the assistance of Europeans left devastated by World War I.

He had arrived in the United States with little in terms of finances, yet his wits and drive made his American landscape a happy one. Luzie's great uncle Nathan typifies the immigrant that American writers and historians point to when speaking of the nation's vibrancy, for he was the quintessential American success story. To his relatives back in Germany, as the Nazis continued to accrue power, he was perhaps their one and only avenue out of the darkness.

May 1933–September 1938

3

First Requests

When Luzie and her father first wrote to Nathan in Albany, New York, in the spring of 1933, it was amid a disturbing string of events. On March 23, only two months after Adolf Hitler had become chancellor, the Nazis maneuvered the Enabling Act through the Reichstag, thereby granting Hitler dictatorial powers. It had taken Hitler little time to transform himself from chancellor to dictator.

Just nine days later, on April 1, German Jewry witnessed the first national boycott of Jewish businesses, products, doctors, and lawyers. "Germans! Defend Yourselves! Do Not Buy from Jews!" This was the common slogan plastered on kiosks and on Jewish store windows, as well as printed on poster boards held by SA troopers standing in front of Jewish businesses.

The German public in general gave the boycott little support, and the Nazi authorities were forced to cancel it after two days. Yet the brevity of the boycott gave little consolation to Luzie's father, who reasoned that this was not the end but the beginning.

A week after the national boycott, on April 7, the Nazis passed the Law for the Restoration of the Professional Civil Service. All Jews as well as anyone deemed "politically unreliable" were to be excluded from state employment. Hitler was rapidly disproving the theory that circumstances would limit his authority.

Such were the conditions facing the Hechts that drove them to request assistance from America. Unfortunately, Luzie did not save her very first letter to her relatives in Albany. Yet the first response, from Uncle Nathan's wife, Ida, *was* saved. It could not have been comforting.

———

To: Luzie Hecht, Berlin
From: Ida Hatch, Albany, New York
Date: May 5, 1933

My Dear Lucie:

So glad you wrote to me in English so that I can answer in the same language. It will be easier for me to express myself than in German in which I am not so fluent. Both Uncle Nathan and I were deeply distressed over your letter and conditions as they now exist in Germany and one might add also all over the world.

I am wondering if you have the slightest idea how sick

Uncle Nathan is. It is now nearly ten months since his operation, and he is still under the care of 2 nurses. God alone knows if and when he will ever get well. He is a broken down old man now (76 years old). I wouldn't want you to see him as he is now but always want you to think of him as you knew him when you last saw him. I am a nervous wreck from grief and worry. You ask my advice, dear Lucie, as to what you should do to improve your condition and your future. My advice is bad as things are in Germany they are not much better here.

What can a German girl do in America just now? When her relatives and friends, experienced and capable, are walking the streets begging and praying for work and can find none. Business is <u>very</u> bad and the Depression has caught us badly. Can't begin to tell you how much.

Uncle Nathan is too sick to really know and his heart aches for you all, and you know full well how gladly he would help you if he could. Everyone in your family appeals to him—Norbert, Martha, Elsa—and he is helpless. Today he is having a very bad day and I am generally worried. Aunt Eda is far from a well woman and has lost a good deal of her money in the Depression. Aunt Alice is almost helpless. So you can see for yourself how conditions are with us. Was pleased to learn your dear mother has recovered her health.

With youth and health you can face the world, but without either you are lost. When Uncle Nathan feels stronger, he will write to your father. Sometimes he has a fairly comfortable day. Please be assured I wish we were in a position to help you. I know advice alone is not what you need or want, but am sorry to say that is all we have to offer at present.

With the hope that you all will continue to enjoy the best of health. With our best love I remain affectionately,

Aunt Ida

———

Just a few days after Luzie's great aunt Ida had penned her response, Nathan gathered enough energy to write his own reply. After his long recovery from surgery, what he refers to as his "43-week-long journey," his response was brief and all too clear.

———

To: Hecht Family, Berlin
From: Nathan Hatch, Albany, New York
Date: May 10, 1933
Translated from the German

My dear family,

It is very difficult for me to write after a 43-week-long journey, and my letter has to be quite short. Either you don't understand the situation here or you don't want to understand it. Business in our company has come to a complete halt. Where we needed 1,000 workers in the past, we now need approximately 150 workers per week today—and let's not even mention profits.

Your intention of coming to America is sheer insanity and you would find the situation horrible. Concerning me: I cannot help you at the present time. You must not under any circumstances rely on me. We are faced with unemployment of 15 million and some have almost no income.

May 1933–September 1938
—
26

In general, I am over 76 years old and am not taking on new burdens, have enough old ones. I am dearly sorry and I hope that better times are ahead. Everyone is waiting.

With love and best wishes,

Your old uncle Nathan

———

First Requests

—

4

Persistence
Rewarded

Nathan Hatch's hope of "better times ahead" never material-
ized. For a short time, it had seemed as though anti-Jewish agitation was slowing, and some Jews who had emigrated made the tragic
mistake of returning to Germany. The Nazi hand grew stronger,
more expansive, and more brutal. The Kristallnacht pogroms are
spoken of as the "watershed" event that made German Jews realize
that emigration was not a choice but an urgent necessity. But even
though those pogroms of November 1938 were the most vicious
attacks on German Jewry to that time, they were hardly the first
such assaults.

Three years earlier, in July 1935, Nazis took to the Kurfürstendamm, the fashionable Berlin street not far from Luzie's neighborhood, smashing the windows of Jewish-owned cafés and restaurants, breaking furniture, and attacking Jewish patrons. The elegant Café Kranzler was among the worst hit. The destruction of Jewish businesses did not satiate the violent appetite of the approximately eight hundred rioters and so passing cars were stopped; "Jewish-looking" passengers were pulled out and thrown to the side of the road or beaten.

Added to outbursts of violence were such "lawful measures" as the Nuremberg Racial Laws of September 1935. Jews were now excluded from Reich citizenship and from marrying or having sexual relations with "Aryans."

And what of April 1936, the very month that Luzie decided to reconnect with the Hatch family in America? Normally a month filled with the joy of both Passover and Easter, that April was colored by occurrences both depressing and bizarre. It was reported that seventy-five thousand German Jews, including twenty-five thousand in Berlin, had received food relief in the form of free matzo.[1] Never before in the history of German Jewry had so many taken Passover relief.

The Easter holiday also had an ignoble distinction that spring. It was the first Easter when Germans could go to market for the holiday and know that they were buying "pure Aryan eggs." *Der Angriff* (The attack), Berlin's Nazi paper, proclaimed that the egg trade, one-fourth Jewish before the Nazis assumed power, was now *Judenrein*, free of Jews.[2]

On April 12, the middle of Passover, the holiday commemorating the Jewish exodus from Egypt, Luzie renewed her efforts to leave Nazi Germany. In the three years since the Hechts had asked Nathan Hatch to help them emigrate, their situation in Germany had worsened. Circumstances had also changed for the Hatch family in America; this time Luzie's request would be sent not to Nathan but to one of his sons.

On June 3, 1933, just four weeks after he had penned his blunt reply to Luzie and her family, Nathan Hatch died. He left behind his wife, Ida, and their two American-born sons, Arnold and Stephen. As the older son, Arnold assumed the presidency of Fuld and Hatch Knitting. His younger brother, Stephen, served as vice president.

Who was Arnold Hatch, this forty-five-year-old man who had simultaneously inherited two large and complex responsibilities: the family business and the issue of how to respond to the needs of his relatives in Nazi Germany? He was, first of all, the son of an ambitious, hardworking entrepreneur with an independent streak. In addition, he had inherited a legacy: his father's numerous civic and philanthropic activities reveal a man with a deep sense of responsibility that extended well beyond his immediate family.

Although Nathan Hatch did not teach his children German, they still had some sense of their German heritage. In 1897, well before Luzie's birth, the family had traveled to Germany for a summer vacation. No doubt this was something of a triumphant return for Nathan, who had left his homeland twenty-four years earlier.

Arnold's one trip to Germany at the young age of nine did not allow the forging of deep bonds between him and his German relatives. Yet it must have provided some tangible link to a place, people, and family history that had formerly been nothing more than names and terms discussed at the dinner table.

When asked for recollections of Arnold, his daughter-in-law, Gloria Hatch, spoke of a big, heavyset, cigar-smoking man who often enjoyed a few drinks before bed, loved to tell jokes and stories, and had many friends. Luzie's cousin Arnold was a man who never seemed to lack confidence. In 1906, he had entered Dartmouth, one of America's most prestigious colleges, only to leave after two years, claiming that he had learned everything they could teach him.

Luzie's immediate family in Berlin, along with other relatives in Essen, Baden, and Cologne, were by definition part of Arnold's extended family. But he had not grown up with them, played childish pranks with his cousins, had his aunts ply him with home-cooked food, shared Passover seders and birthdays, or made visits to sick family members. All of these experiences, events that weave the threads of strong family bonds, were missing. Yet even without these everyday contacts, at some level, his German relatives had become part of his consciousness. And so he did respond to Luzie when she first wrote to him, even though they had never corresponded before. She knew so little about him that she inquired whether he was married and had children.

When Luzie wrote her cousin Arnold asking him to bring her to America, she did so in secret, not telling her parents. After their disappointing experience in 1933, perhaps Edwin and Helene had decided that this avenue of escape was closed, that another attempt would only have angered their Albany relatives. Luzie, however, decided to be persistent, to try once more.

It is likely that not a day passed when Luzie didn't wonder about Arnold's response. After all, he was Nathan's son. Would he be as opposed to her emigration as his father had been? Even worse, might her request go unanswered? But Arnold did respond. Nearly a month from the day she mailed her request, his reply arrived in Berlin; given the mail system, he had been rather prompt.

We can only guess what Luzie's reaction was on the day the letter arrived at 12 Zähringerstrasse. Did she quickly rip it open?

Or is it more likely instead that she retreated to her bedroom, nervously turning the letter over and over again before gathering the courage to open it and doing so carefully so as not to tear one precious word?

———

To: Lusie Hecht, Berlin
From: Arnold Hatch, Albany, New York
Date: April 23, 1936

Dear Lusie:

I have received your letter dated April 12th and I can appreciate how little prospect there is in the future for a girl of ambition, situated as you are. I should very much like to help you in the way that you mention, and will try to see what can be done.

However, there are certain things that you should bear in mind. One of these is that the Depression which is afflicting Germany to a certain extent at this time is worldwide and has hit America very hard. There are in this country today between 10,000,000 and 12,000,000 unemployed, and these include plenty of people of ability and training who are willing to work at almost any job and almost any salary. I have countless friends struggling along on little or nothing, thrown out of work by reason of economic conditions here and unable to find anything which will even give them a bare substinence.

A good many people abroad have the idea that jobs are easy and plentiful in this country, but I assure you that this is not the case and I would hardly know where to turn right at this minute to find a post for you suitable to your training and abilities, which would even give you a living.

In addition, there is the question of the American immigration quota. Under this, as you probably understand, only a limited number of Germans are allowed into this country and since thousands of people are in the same position that you are, anxious to get out of Germany and into a land of greater promise, I have an idea that the quota is pretty much filled up.

You must not get the idea from what I have written so far that I am simply turning a deaf ear to your plea and tossing your letter aside forever. I shall really look into this thing carefully and see if there is any position where you could be placed in this country later on this summer. If I could receive some assurance that you would have something waiting for you when you got here, I would very gladly furnish the necessary affidavits to enable you to assure the immigration authorities that you would not become a public charge and would do all I could to help you get in under the German quota.

Of course, there is no use in saying right now come along as fast as you can, because that would be reckless and foolish and unwise for both of us. However, I think that a girl of your intelligence, education and training should have a chance, and I am not unmindful of the fact that you are a blood relative and are entitled to my help out of sentiment for your dear grandfather, whom I remember well.

In conclusion then I want you to let this matter rest a while until I can see what I can do for you. It will not be easy and in the end it may turn out to be impossible, but if

Persistence Rewarded

—

there is a chance in the world that I can take you out of Germany and help you build a new life in this land; I give you my promise that I will do it.

I would suggest that you talk this matter fully over with your father, because there is no sense in secrecy over this and not the slightest reason why you should not have written to me and asked me to help you in your problem. I am glad that you did write to me and as I said before, if there is any possibility of bringing you over here so that you can be reasonably secure, self-supporting, and with a future, I will send for you, execute any papers that may be necessary, and help you in every possible manner. In the meanwhile, my dear cousin, with my sincere love to you and your family, I am

Your devoted cousin,
Arnold

———

Although Arnold had stated that he needed time to investigate the matter of emigration properly, his response had been quite positive overall and must have been reassuring to Luzie. Slightly less than two years later, in the winter of 1938, the one letter from Albany that Luzie had always hoped for finally arrived in Berlin.

———

To: Lusie Hecht, Berlin
From: Arnold Hatch, Albany, New York
Date: February 8, 1938

Dear Cousin Lusie:

The time has now come after almost a year's delay when

I am prepared to bring you over to this country. I am starting measures at once through the American Consul to vouch for you, and while these things take several months, nevertheless, the matter is being started, and I wanted to inform you of that fact so that you could at least begin to set your house in order and make preparations for coming to this country.

This does not mean that you would be wise to give up your present job or do anything at all until the German Consul notifies you that matters are arranged. You can simply begin thinking about it because I am willing and have agreed to it.

I do not know how you are fixed financially. If you are unable to finance for yourself the trip across, I should be only too glad to do so for you, when the time comes. Once you are in this country, I may be able to get you a job . . . However, whether you get a job immediately or not, I will look after you and see that you are not in want or in trouble in any way.

There is no need to write at greater length now. I know that you will be happy that I have finally agreed to what you have wanted so long. Later on, when things get nearer the time for your departure, we will arrange all matters . . .

I extend to you and your family my love and hope that everything is well with you.

Your devoted cousin,

Arnold

———

To: Arnold Hatch, Albany, New York
From: Lusie Hecht, Berlin
Date: February 28, 1938

Dear Cousin Arnold!

I have received your very nice letter of February 8th and can hardly express my gladness about the contents of it.

At present I only can thank you with words for all that you intend to do for me, but I hope that once in the future I can prove you my thankfulness and can show you that I never will forget your kindness.

I will be very anxious to find a job as soon as I am over there so that you have no trouble with me. According to your instructions I don't give up my job or do anything at all until the German Consul notifies me that matters are arranged.

I am awaiting your further good news, and in the meantime I'll take many English lessons in order to speak perfectly. If you know some work wanted in America that I can learn too, I would be thankful for your information, so that I can do all to make me fit in every respect.

your very thankful cousin,

Lusie

To: Lusie Hecht, Berlin
From: Arnold Hatch, Albany, New York
Date: March 8, 1938

Dear Cousin Lusie:

I have your letter of February 28, and first of all I do

not believe that I informed you previously that in addition to you, I am bringing over here your cousin Herta Stein who is the daughter of Elsa Stein, from Berkach. All papers in connection with you two girls have been completed and are on the way to the American Consul abroad.

You of course understand that from now on, the speed with which this goes forward is out of my control, but I imagine that things will move along pretty well and that it will not be a great while before you are asked to appear before the American Consul for examination and investigation.

I think I may be able to find a job for you when you arrive in this country or at least help you secure one but whether you get one or not, I will see that you are taken care of until you are employed. In the meanwhile, you might be making some inquiries about what your expenses will be in marks, to get to this country. We will send you the money and you need not worry about whether you have enough of your own or whether you can secure an advance or loan from anyone else.

All you have to do from now on is to keep me informed about how this matter is progressing and give me as much advance information as possible about when you are called on by the Consul and approximately when you think you could leave Germany.

In the meanwhile, my best love to you and your family and you need not worry about a thing.

Your devoted cousin,
Arnold

Encouraged by Luzie's success, Edwin Hecht once again reached out to his Albany relative. Arnold replied promptly, explaining his situation.

To: Edwin Hecht, Berlin
From: Arnold Hatch, Albany, New York
Date: August 13, 1938

Dear Cousin Edwin:

I received your letter written on the 20th of July with a postscript added from your wife, Helene, and I think that I realize the difficulties that you are facing today. However, I am unable to comply with your request at the present time. Regardless of the necessity of coming to America and your willingness to work at anything while here, it is not easy to secure employment in this country at the present time, although most foreigners do not seem to realize that.

I do not want to bring over any of the relatives unless I have a pretty definite idea what to do with them when they get here. By that, I mean that I must have some sort of employment either definitely arranged or in prospect. That is the situation with the two girls, Lusie and Herta. Herta, of course, will live with Aunts Eda and Alice and look after them, and as for Lusie, I had a job arranged for her in an office in New York. This is what I mean when I say that I have to have things arranged before I can bring people over here.

You may or may not know that I have had requests similar to yours from literally dozens of our relatives in

Germany—some of them whom I cannot even place in my memory. It is a matter of regret that most of these have to be turned down or rejected, but regardless of the situation, there is a limit to the responsibility that I can assume, and there is no one else over here who can or will assume any.

Perhaps, at some future time, something can be done. I assure you that I will talk this over fully and carefully with Lusie when I see her. When I can see my way clear to bring you to this country so that your life here will not be all at loose ends, I shall do so.

> Yours very truly,
> Arnold

———

Finally, in the fall of 1938, plans were finalized for Luzie and Herta's departure. In this letter, one of his last, Arnold enclosed a small, passport-size photo of himself so that Luzie could identify him when she disembarked. A close look at this photo reveals its many creases. It had had a good deal of wear. No doubt Luzie had looked at it again and again while on ship and held onto it for dear life when she arrived in Manhattan.

———

To: Lusie Hecht, Berlin
From: Arnold Hatch, Albany, New York
Date: September 13, 1938

Dear Cousin Lusie:

This will acknowledge receipt of your letter dated September 4th. I am sorry if I neglected to answer your letter of July 13th. This was purely an oversight.

I am glad that the matter of the physical examinations, the visas, etc., is progressing satisfactorily, and I feel quite confidant that nothing will materialize to prevent your sailing on the contemplated date.

I will meet that steamer when it comes in. There is enclosed a small photograph of me, which will perhaps be useful in aiding you to identify me. So that you will not be frightened, I might add that I am not always as angry as it would appear from this picture.

With much love to you all, I am your devoted cousin,

Arnold

———

May 1933–September 1938

PART TWO

December 1938–
August 1939

5

Settling In

A New Life in New York

Luzie and her cousin Herta Stein boarded the *Manhattan,* a steamer bound for New York, on November 16, 1938, just one week after the Kristallnacht pogroms. They were leaving in the wake of a nightmare, well described in the Jewish Telegraphic Agency's wire:

> An estimated 25,000 Jews were under arrest here today in the wake of the worst outbreak of anti-Jewish violence in modern German history, which left throughout the nation a trail of burned synagogues, smashed homes, wrecked and pillaged shops, and at least four known dead. Police seizures

of Jews continued throughout the night and this morning.
Three thousand were in custody in Berlin alone . . .

Throughout the city [Berlin] hardly a single Jewish
shop or restaurant window was left intact as bands pro-
ceeded systematically from street to street, smashing panes
with hammers and stoning those beyond reach.[1]

The violence and pillaging that occurred in Berlin was repeated in
Jewish communities large and small throughout Germany.

Those fourteen hours of rioting and destruction were a bolt that
struck the consciousness of German Jews, making it impossible to
cling to any notion, any fantasy that they could somehow accommodate themselves to the Nazi regime, that it would eventually become more moderate, and that Germany could still be their home.

After nine days at sea, Luzie Hecht arrived at her new home
on November 16. She would write of landing in New York on the
afternoon of a very clear day, standing on the ship's deck and looking out at the vast metropolis of New York City with its truly commanding skyscrapers. Like many newcomers, Luzie would be struck
by the city's vastness, quick pace, and energy.

Learning her way around Manhattan would be just one of
many tasks she faced. There was much to do: find a job, improve
her English, and most important, get her family out of Germany.
Having witnessed those "terrible days," Luzie knew they couldn't
stay in Berlin. She understood full well that emigration had become
the only option.

In addition, there was the pressing issue of her cousin Herta's
father, her uncle Salomon, age fifty-three. Salomon Stein had been
among the thousands of Jewish men rounded up during Kristallnacht and transported to concentration camps. Release from hellish

camps such as Sachsenhausen was possible if the internee could provide proof of his plans to leave Germany. This evidence, of course, had to be gathered by relatives or friends on the outside.

As Arnold would often tell Luzie, she was the older one, the city girl, more experienced than her country cousin, and fluent in English. So it was not Herta, Salomon's daughter, but Luzie who was assigned the responsibility for his fate. It was Luzie who wrote to Arnold asking him to fill out the necessary forms, on Salomon's behalf, and to cable them to Germany. There were many letters to exchange.

To: Luzie Hecht, New York
From: Arnold Hatch, Albany, New York
Date: December 5, 1938

Dear Luzie:

I have your letter of December 3rd, and I shall prepare and sign the affidavits as quickly as possible and send them to you. There will be a little delay in this because it is necessary to accumulate from income tax auditors, banks, life insurance companies, etc., the necessary proofs, and this will take a few days . . .

Now, as regards the cables, I am sending these at once, and the only possible good that they can do is perhaps to release Salomon Stein from a concentration camp and to prevent your father from getting in one. Personally, I think these cables are a mistake at this stage of the proceedings. However, I am sending them anyway in the hope that they will do some good and at least give some comfort to the two families in question.

Regardless of all the foregoing, on which we are going ahead, I very much fear that it is going to be a terribly long-winded proposition to get your parents and Rolf, and also Herta's parents, out of Germany. From everything that I can ascertain, the signing of the affidavits means that you simply start the ball rolling ... Nevertheless, we shall do our best, and no one can do more than that.

I would suggest that as soon as possible that you call on Miss Celia Razovsky, c/o National Coordinating Committee for German Refugees, 165 West 46th Street, New York City, and have a talk with this lady. She is perhaps the best posted woman that I know of on the extremely complicated conditions that prevail today ... Obviously, you can see that a great deal more can be done toward starting this by you in New York than by me in Cohoes.

I think that you are entirely wrong that the signing of these affidavits will immediately release a man from a concentration camp. However, if you are right and I am wrong about this, I am perfectly willing not merely to sign the affidavits but to cable them if that will help.

So get busy, as we say in America, and see what you can do at your end.

Your devoted cousin,
Arnold

———

Right from the start, Luzie's cousin Arnold made one thing clear. There was a difference between being charitable and being a pushover, and he certainly was not the latter.

December 1938–August 1939
———

46

To: Luzie Hatch, New York

From: Arnold Hatch, Albany, New York

Date: December 8, 1938

Dear Luzie:

I talked to my brother Stephen on the phone today and was somewhat surprised at several of the things he told me. Among these was your intimation that the money I gave you in New York was gone.

He also stated that you moved and simply abandoned the deposit left with Mrs. Rose. Now that original room was not too desirable, but it could have been made to do until the deposit left with the lady was used up. I must insist right at the beginning that when you do things of this kind that you consult with me and not simply go ahead on your own initiative and without regard to expense or what others may think.

It will be my responsibility to look after you until you are able to find a job and support yourself, but you will have to consult with me about things and not just do as you please, move where you please, and live as you please, without regard to expense. Money is as important here just the same as it is in Germany and is not to be squandered.

Now, as regards a job. It is true that finding a job is not easy, but perhaps it is still more difficult to find just the sort of a job that you think you are entitled to have. Right at this time of year with all the stores putting on Christmas help and with your selling experience, I should imagine that you could find something to do, unless you have arrived at the conclusion that only a certain type of dignified job will do for you.

If you have been unable to find anything by the time you get this letter, you will find enclosed a letter addressed to the man in charge of my sales office in New York, Mr. Horace M. Graff. I want you to take this letter down to him at 93 Worth Street, and he will help you as much as he can.

Now, it is not my intention to be mean or petty or miserly with you because that is not my way at all, but you must not get any false ideas about things right at the beginning of your life in America. I object very strenuously to your proceeding about a lot of things without consulting me, and when I feel strongly about anything I say so.

Now, get busy and see if you cannot place yourself, and instead of all this intimation about how you are broke, how you are planning to sell your fur coat, how you are blue and discouraged about finances, just write me the facts from time to time, and I will see that you do not want for anything as long as you live simply, economically, and wisely.

Yours, as ever,

Arnold

———

In all likelihood, Arnold's letter sparked worry and perhaps even fear in Luzie's mind. After all, she and her family were dependent on Arnold. What if he washed his hands of them? Who would bring Edwin, Helene, and Ralph Hecht to the United States? The thought that her family could perish, leaving Luzie a single woman in a new land, could not have been comforting.

December 1938–August 1939
———

Had Arnold been too harsh with Luzie? A refugee from Germany, she had been in the United States for all of thirteen days, twelve if one subtracts the Thanksgiving holiday, when no job efforts could be made, and he wanted to know why she was not yet working. Thousands of native-born Americans who had no language problems, could easily navigate their city, were familiar with local business customs, and had relatives and friends to assist them were also without work in 1938. If this argument crossed Luzie's mind, she certainly knew enough not to raise it with Arnold.

It was not simply her unemployed status that was irritating Arnold. There were also her spending habits. As Arnold saw it, after having been careless with money, his cousin now needed to sell her precious possessions. But her fur coat and jewelry were, in fact, a portable bank account in disguise. Back in Berlin, facing Nazi restrictions on how much cash she could take out of Germany, Luzie had purchased expensive goods for the express purpose of converting them to cash in New York. Although the Nazis would eventually clamp down on such actions, when Luzie left this method of circumvention still worked. Selling these articles was not the result of careless spending—on the contrary, it was all part of Luzie's plan. All of this needed to be explained in her reply.

To: Arnold Hatch, Albany, New York
From: Luzie Hatch, New York
Date: December 11, 1938

Dear Cousin Arnold:

I noted the contents of your letter of December 8th quite carefully and am so awfully sad that evidently when meeting your brother Stephen I didn't use the right words so that a big misunderstanding occurred.

First of all I want you to be assured that until now I had always to live simply, economically and wisely and that I <u>never</u> intended to live here in another manner. On the contrary I never spend a cent if it is not necessary.

I took this room only with the intention to stay about two weeks until I get accustomed to the life of New York, as a married girlfriend from Berlin lives in the next house and could help me to overcome the first difficulties. My cousin Edith, you met her at the steamer, has now her own apartment and is willing to give me a very nice and clean room with breakfast for $5.—a week. I already intended to change today to the 162nd street, but as I really don't want to do anything without consulting you, I should like you to let me know whether you think this all right and agree to it.

Stephen asked me whether I need money, and I answered that I already spent a lot, but that I have enough. So he said I should write to you if I am low in funds, and I told him before writing I would prefer to sell my jewelry and my fur coat as for this special purpose I bought these things in Germany.

I am not at all discouraged, but as now I am accustomed a little more to all those things I didn't know before, I feel quite happy and hope quite confidentially that I find a job within the next time.

I thank you very much for your letter to Mr. Horace M. Graff but, if you don't mind, I would prefer to try to place myself before I go to him. I had the intention to visit some people on Friday, but the whole day I was occupied with

December 1938–August 1939

sending the affidavits abroad. Tomorrow after having visited the Committee, I shall go to different places and hope that there will be a chance for me. Also on Tuesday and Wednesday I'll try to find work and let you know the results at once.

Dear Cousin Arnold, please be convinced that I <u>really don't live without regard to expense,</u> and please be so kind to show your brother Stephen this letter, so that any other misunderstanding will be avoided.

Yours, as ever,

Luzie

————

————

To: Luzie Hecht, New York

From: Arnold Hatch, Albany, New York

Date: December 12, 1938

Dear Luzie:

I haven't much time to write you at length today as I have to go to a bank meeting in Albany. The room that you mention with your cousin, Edith Friedmann, sounds attractive, and I would recommend that you take that as soon as possible.

In the meanwhile, I do not want you to sell any jewelry or furs. When your money is gone or low, let me know definitely, and I shall send you some more and maintain you suitably until you are able to find a job.

You should make every effort to place yourself in a job as quickly as possible, and I do not mind if you postpone going to see Mr. Graff until you have tried elsewhere.

Settling In

—

However, the matter should not be delayed longer than necessary.

With much love to you and Herta and our two aunts, I am

Yours, as ever,

Arnold

Luzie's most pressing task was to secure the essential affidavits of financial support for both her family and Herta's parents. With hundreds of thousands unemployed, the last thing the US government wanted was additional people in need of assistance. Those with meager funds thus needed an affidavit of financial support to secure their visas.

By the beginning of December, after having been in New York for just twelve days, Luzie was successful. The papers documenting Arnold's sponsorship of both families were sent to Berlin through the office of the National Coordinating Committee for German Refugees. Getting the paperwork through was an exhausting ordeal, accomplished only after overcoming a number of obstacles.

To: Arnold Hatch, Albany, New York

From: Luzie Hatch, New York

Date: December 10, 1938

Dear Cousin Arnold:

Please accept Herta's and my best thanks for sending the affidavits for our families.

When I received your letter of December 8th, I went at once to the Committee. The employees were very busy, and

I was sent from one room to the other. At last I got a girl who informed me that she had to go right away and that I had to come again.

You can imagine that I was very anxious to send the affidavits abroad with the *Aquitania* sailing today and therefore offered her to write the necessary letters myself at home, if she gives me their letter-paper. After long hesitation, as she is not allowed to do so, she agreed, and I hurried home.

In the afternoon, when I was ordered again she told me that she has to disappoint me as I got the wrong letter-paper, and then again I was sent to different rooms. Nobody had time to help me as it was already very late, and as the office is closed on Saturday and Sunday, I had to find a way out of this trouble.

After having waited a long time, I informed the secretary that I would be able to write the letters myself right there (the other girl had forbidden that I say anything about my writing at home), so at last they gave me the right letter-paper and in a big typewriter-room I wrote the letters.

The affidavits were sent to the American Consul in Berlin, and our parents got a letter from the Committee with copy of the letter to the Consul.

I hope now to receive good news from our parents and thank you again for giving them the possibility of building a new life.

Your cousin
Luzie

———

Luzie still faced the pressing challenge of finding employment.

—

To: Arnold Hatch, Albany, New York

From: Luzie Hecht, New York

Date: December 12, 1938

Dear Cousin Arnold:

Today I visited several firms. I had luck in meeting the President of Messrs. Edward P. Paul & Co., Inc. I know him already from his trips to Germany, and he was very nice to me.

They don't need any employee at all, but as he wants very much to help me, he is ready to create an additional position for me. He told me that I could come and he would pay me for the beginning $12.00 dollars a week. I had to write two letters after dictation, and he was satisfied with my work.

Now $12.00 is very little, but if I don't find another job I'll take this if you find it alright. If I don't earn so much at the beginning, I have at least the occasion to learn American business methods, and this is very important for me. Please let me know your opinion.

Just now Herta informs me that she got a telegram from home that her father came out of the concentration camp, and of course she is now very happy.

With best regards to you and Stephen, also to your wife,

I am,

Luzie

—

December 1938–August 1939

—

54

Luzie accepted the office job at Messrs. Edward P. Paul and Company for twelve dollars a week. Unfortunately, her employment there was short-lived—just the two remaining weeks of the Christmas season. She was probably apprehensive about telling Arnold that she was once again among the unemployed. However, Arnold responded with a pleasant surprise: a check for twenty-five dollars along with consoling words: "Now, do not feel blue or discouraged. These things happen to everyone, and the position that you lost was not too marvelous an opportunity anyway."

She had learned an important lesson about her American-born cousin. As long as he received the proper respect and thought that she, on her side, was making every effort to adjust and work hard, he would be not only generous but warm.

Luzie was clearly someone who liked to be in charge, get things done, and have matters under control. After all, in a matter of days, she had acquired and sent the affidavits of support to Germany. But neither she nor her successful American cousin had any power over the insufficient German immigration quota.

In 1939, the US Immigration Service set the German quota at just slightly over twenty-seven thousand. Given the desperation of German Jews to flee Nazi rule, that number was painfully inadequate.

Luzie's father, Edwin, was among the thousands of anxious Jews who had applied for immigration at the US consulate in Berlin. He may even have applied before Kristallnacht. The Hechts had been assigned a number so high it would not be called for years. Yet given the terror that now enveloped the Jewish community, the waiting period could not be spent in Germany.

Edwin Hecht was fortunate enough to be able to buy passenger tickets for the one place in the world open to Jewish refugees.

He, Helene, and Ralph would head for Shanghai. Here in this bustling port city, they would wait for their turn to come to America.

For many years, Luzie and her cousin Arnold had gone through life knowing next to nothing about each other. In dealing with this crisis, however, even though their communication was rarely face-to-face, usually by letters, and only occasionally by phone, they were quickly getting to know each other. Luzie must have known from the start, even before discussing her father's decision with Arnold, that he would be irate. His first question would surely be, "How will they ever survive in Shanghai?" Arnold was not alone in his concern about the Hechts' future in Shanghai. Luzie also had her worries.

Seeking a different solution, she wrote to a dear family friend, Arnold Godschalk, who had owned a toy business in Germany and had had the good fortune of relocating his family to London. Perhaps somehow he could help her family get to England and spare them the dangers and hardships of Shanghai.

———

To: Arnold Godschalk, London
From: Luzie Hatch, New York
Date: January 18, 1939
Translated from the German

Dear Arnold,

We haven't heard from each other in a long time, and I hope that you and your dear family are doing well.

I have been in the "country of unlimited opportunities" since November 27, 1938, and of course very glad to be able to breathe again and be a free person. But along with being here other problems have arisen. While I had succeeded in finding temporary employment, at the moment I am again out of work and have been unable to find a new job. The competition here is terribly high.

New immigrants arrive every day, all of whom get stuck here and naturally also want to find work. I would very much like to go elsewhere in the country, but haven't received the right offers yet, and then I have so much here that I need to take care of for my parents that I cannot leave yet.

As you can imagine, they [parents and brother] cannot possibly remain in Germany. What I experienced there is indescribable. After much persuasion, I succeeded at arranging for my relatives to file the affidavit for all three, father, mother, and Rolf, which was already sent to Berlin in early December. As you know, it will take a certain amount of time before they can immigrate to the United States.

But since it is just impossible to spend this waiting period in Berlin, they have now made plans to go to Shanghai. The local committee that I approached for advice strongly discourages going to Shanghai, as the conditions there are said to be appalling. I wrote this to my parents immediately and begged them to seek out another route.

One hears generally that under certain circumstances, immigrants who are in possession of an American affidavit can spend the waiting period in England. And I would be exceedingly grateful if you could inquire about this and report back to me, should your schedule permit.

I certainly wouldn't bother you if it wasn't such a serious problem and if I myself wasn't so perplexed. My parents think that because I am here, I can do everything for them, but they forget that I myself haven't quite warmed up here, and can't even feed myself.

I have urgently advised my parents to send Rolf to England or Holland via student transportation. He will then have to remain in one of those countries until he can come here. I know that it will be very difficult for my parents to give the boy away, but at the moment, one must take advantage of every opportunity.

It is a horrible situation.

I would be very thankful to you if you could answer me soon.

Have you settled in well in the meantime? And are you satisfied with business?

Please remember me to your wife and greetings to you too, from

Yours,

Luzie

———

———

To: Luzie Hatch, New York

From: Arnold Godschalk, London

Date: February 7, 1939

Dear Luzie,

I am in receipt of your letter of the 18th January, and have been surprised and at the same time glad, to hear from you in New York.

No doubt it is not so easy to find the job you are looking for but, on the other hand, I think it is far better making even a small living and being in a free country.

I have had heaps of letters from Germany, asking me for help. Unfortunately, I have had to set a limit to these things. The most important part in helping people from Germany is financial, but besides that, even if one is able to put down the necessary deposit, it still takes a very long time and lots of trouble to be successful.

As for your parents, if they want to come to England, they need a guarantor who gives the Government the necessary guarantee that he is going to be responsible for them during their stay in England. If your family in New York is in the financial position to make a deposit (about £200.0.0 is needed). They should get in touch with one of the Refugee Committees here, but without any financial security, it is absolutely out of the question.

I like the country, but business is still very difficult. I am still more or less starting, but hope for the best.

It seems a long while ago since we met in "Preussen Park" on a Sunday morning.

With best regards,

Yours,

Arnold Godschalk

———

Although Luzie's immediate family was still struggling to escape Germany, some in her extended family had already fled. Cousins Werner, Ilse, and Kate had left for the Netherlands. Thousands of Germans resettled in the Netherlands and France, believing they had escaped the Nazis. In fact, they had found only a temporary breathing space. When Hitler's armies marched into these countries in May 1940, they would once again be under the Nazi boot. However, in the winter of 1939, when Luzie sat down to write her cousins, she mistakenly believed that they, too, had found safety.

To: Luzie's cousins, the Netherlands
From: Luzie Hecht, New York
Date: February 9, 1939
Translated from the German

Dear all!

Father wrote me you were surprised that you have not yet heard from me—you would not wonder any longer if you had seen the bustle here. Regardless of my silence, I have certainly not forgotten you. I have now settled in a little bit and have gotten used to the new, so that I find the time to speak to you at length again.

With my parents it is difficult, unfortunately. They have come to the decision to go to Shanghai on the 21st of this month. Arnold is absolutely against this enterprise, just as the committees strongly discourage it, since Shanghai is located in the middle of a battle zone and suffers from an excessive number of all kinds of refugees anyhow, and besides it provides no opportunity to earn money. In other words, it would mean jumping out of the frying pan and into the fire. At Arnold's instigation, I have therefore cabled my parents again this week, saying they should make up a different plan and hope strongly that yet another way can be found.

It is an awful condition, all countries shut down, and in Germany they cannot feel confident about their lives. I have also tried to get help from friends in England and the Netherlands, so that they can at least stay in these countries temporarily, but everything still is very uncertain. My hands are tied as well. I am without work for weeks now and cannot even feed myself.

———

Not wanting merely to send a short note but pressed for time, she put this letter aside, picking it up again two months later.

———

April 20th, 1939

Although most of what I have written on the prior page about two months ago is vastly outdated now, I do want to attach it in order to assure you of the good "intentions," i.e., giving you a detailed report.

You should be very happy that all of you are together. All of you can breathe a sigh of relief. Do you, dear Herta, have employment, or is it not allowed to work without a permit in the Netherlands?

That is what is so nice here. One can start to work from day one after immigrating legally—even though it is very tough to find a position. The situation here is dreadful at the moment. I really thought only millionaires would be running around, and I was greatly disillusioned. Just when I began to be desperate, I found a position at a committee

[American Jewish Committee] seven weeks ago. I get paid relatively well and work only five days a week, so that I can relax and recover nicely over the weekend.

You, dear Werner, know I enjoy working and that I am used to doing it for 10 years now, but for the time being everything is more exhausting to me than it was in Germany, since I am not quite adjusted to the climate. None of us is accustomed to such changes in temperature and climate, as they appear here between the mornings and evenings, and it does take a while until the body changes over to it.

I worry only about the heat that is to come soon. The most unpleasant aspect is supposedly not the heat itself, but the air that has such a high percentage of humidity that one is constantly wet. Well, what millions can bear I should be able to endure, too—and regardless of the many differences and the many adjustments I have to go through, I am happy and content to be here, day after day.

However, one is very worried about the fate of the others who were left back, and besides, the constant war psychosis is annoying. One does not know what to wish for, better an end with horror, while all of us want to wish and hope that horror will befall the other side, than this constant horror without an end.

I often eat at Edith's. First of all she charges me little, and also I'd rather eat the old familiar food. I am not quite used to the American type, which is different (just like the people are much more diverse and different than I have ever imagined).

I have not yet seen too much of New York, unfortunately, because I do not have much time on my hands. When I did not work, I ran around looking for a position from dusk till dawn and came home dead tired and exhausted, and now I am strained from work again, and then I also have many acquaintances. So every day and evening there is something else to do, even if it is only laundry and ironing, so that I do not lack occupation; just to the contrary, I effectively do not have the time to take care of everything I want to do.

For instance, it is very important that I attend an evening school at night, in order to improve my English. I did indeed understand almost everybody and everything from the first day I arrived and am able to chat fluently, but one notices daily how far away one is from being perfect. Well, for my own comfort I tell myself that I am here only for a short time now and that therefore I should not be in a rush.

I hear little from our cousins here. We were welcomed warmly and I was in Albany over Christmas, but other than that I see them every two months at the most. Both of them are very fine and nice, but real Americans. You do not notice that they have had a German father at all.

What other interesting things do you know? Please write me in such detail as I did tonight, I am interested in everything, also in how relatives, friends, and acquaintances are doing who are not yet out [of Germany] and whom you know about.

Well, now I really have to close. "Queen Mary" should receive more mail from me, which yet needs to be produced.

Settling In

I ask for a notice from all the family members whether this letter was detailed enough and if you were pleased with my report.

To all of you, all the best and sincere regards and kisses.

Luzie

———

More Than Friends

During the war years, Luzie would receive many pleas for assistance. Most would come from relatives, but not all. In the winter of 1939, there was a desperate appeal from the Friedländer family, the Hecht family's former upstairs neighbors. The Friedländers, Hechts, and Simons had been a tight-knit group at 12 Zähringerstrasse, gathering each week to play a card game called skat. The rise of Nazism had cast these families in three very different directions. With close relatives in the United States, the Simons were the first to leave, settling in New York. For the Friedländers, too, as for most German Jews, America was the preferred destination. Lacking any close American contacts, however, they were compelled to look elsewhere on the map.

In the days after Kristallnacht, Herbert Friedländer gathered his money and passport and boarded the train for Hamburg, the location of many foreign consulates and embassies. "The Jewish people," his daughter, Inge, recalls, "always talked to each other. There is something here. A possibility here. So he went to the Uruguayan consulate and he bought visas. Ok, he bought visas. That's what you did at the time."[2] As soon as he returned to Berlin, he purchased ship tickets. The Friedländers now had their lifeline: visas and a passage to Montevideo.

Yet even with these precious documents, they faced the dangers of everyday life in Nazi Germany. Answering a knock on the door one evening, Herbert's wife, Paula, was shocked to face members of the Gestapo. They had come for Herbert, who fortunately was not in. Aiming to prevent future visits, Paula pointed to the packed suitcases and explained that they were leaving Germany. For safety, Herbert spent the next few nights in the home of non-Jewish friends.

Amid the hurried packing, selling what they could, saying their good-byes, and avoiding the Gestapo, the family never stopped to imagine their new life in far-off South America. "It was just a way out," remarks Inge Friedländer. "There was no thinking how it would be. It was out, out of Germany. That was all that mattered."[3]

Once on the ship and bound for Uruguay, the family finally had a chance, if not to relax a bit, at least to shake off some nervousness and fear. For the teenaged Inge, the ship passage was a "good time." There were people of her age, particularly young, attractive men, a whole mix of people with whom she could socialize. But as Herbert Friedländer wrote in this letter to Luzie, their plans to settle in Uruguay went terribly wrong.

To: All

From: Herbert and Inge Friedländer, Bahia, Brazil

Date: March 3, 1939

Translated from the German

Dear all!

You might have heard of our fate; we are in great despair; we are unable to land in Montevideo; the visas have

Settling In

—

65

been denied. We then had to go to Buenos Aires, where we were held in custody and could not leave the ship for 10 days, and later had to go back. They strung us along with promises from day to day. There were negotiations with Chile and Bolivia, but nothing worked out. Now we are facing the worst: going back.

We now ask you to try everything, so that we can at least get a temporary asylum in the U.S. or someplace else, because we are despairing. We are on the ship *General San Martin* and will arrive in Madeira on the 29th, in Lisbon on the 31st. Please do everything in your power, otherwise we are lost. Paulchen [Paula] is in a dreadful mental state; please excuse her not writing, she says hello.

How are you? Hopefully you are always well! Could one have expected such a thing when leaving Berlin!

We hope you can achieve something for us, and warm regards.

Your Herbert

———

Unfortunately, nothing in Luzie's correspondence or papers suggests that she was able to help the Friedländers. Most likely they were simply added to her growing list of worries. But in another case, that of a business contact named Stefan Pauson, who with his brother ran a basket business in Bamberg, Germany, the outcome would be different.

As an L. S. Mayer staffer, Luzie probably met Stefan Pauson at the biannual Leipzig Trade Fair. For seven to ten days every March and August, Leipzig hummed with the bustle of thousands of merchants and businesspeople from all over Europe as they eagerly reestablished contact with regular customers, secured new clients, and took stock of the business climate.

Luzie's correspondence makes it clear that she knew not only Pauson but also his teenage daughter Hella, who had joined her father on his final trip to the trade fair. "My sister," Eva Emmerich recalls, "was at the age where she wanted to see the world and meet people, so he took her along to Leipzig."[4] In all likelihood, this last trip to the trade show had been in August 1938; three months later, the Kristallnacht pogroms and the accompanying anti-Jewish legislation would have made it nearly impossible for a German Jew to attend the fair.

Unlike Luzie's father, Edwin, who had escaped the Nazis' noose during Kristallnacht, Stefan Pauson was at home when the troopers rapped on his door. Sent to Dachau, for four to five weeks he struggled to fend off cold, hunger, and constant degradation and fear. "They had to go out in the cold and exercise and if they couldn't handle it, if they collapsed or complained they just beat them to death and that was the end of them," explains his daughter Eva. "So he learned very soon, you do the best you can and you put up with it and you don't make a sound complaining because then you'll never go home."[5]

Newspapers, if an internee could get a hold of them, served a new purpose in Dachau; tucked under one's clothes as insulation, they could provide extra warmth. But there was nothing Pauson could do about the woefully inadequate diet. Like so many Jewish men imprisoned during Kristallnacht, he returned home emaciated, a piercing shock to the family member who opened the door. "My mother," Eva remembers, "was desperately trying to feed him but he couldn't eat the food. He had to eat a real [special] diet to get his stomach and system working again."[6]

With time, Pauson regained his health, and in March 1939, he and his wife and older daughter Hella were able to leave Germany for England to join their younger children, Eva and Peter, who had emigrated about five weeks earlier. In this letter to Luzie, Pauson expressed his appreciation for her help in his efforts to leave Germany.

From: Stefan Pauson, Leicester, England

To: Luzie Hatch, New York

Date: March 24, 1939

Dear Miss "Hatch"

Gratitude certainly isn't one of the most pervasive virtues. Hence, as I can see, until now no one has thanked you yet for your tremendous efforts on my behalf. And therefore I would like to do so myself, even though it was already back on December 10th I managed to crawl out of Dachau, but only since March 13th that I am out of the accursed German Reich.

In any case, you might be interested to know that, although it is not certain whether it actually helped to expedite the permit, your letter lies in the files of the British Home Office as a historic document on the perfidy of the Germans.

That your parents and most likely also your brother are safely out of that country of thugs must surely be a relief to you, although I'm afraid that Shanghai is not quite the ideal.

I requested your address, also for Hella [daughter], received it and then misplaced it again. My brother, who spent a long time looking for a job, is now busier than he would like to be and is a sort of manager at a wicker furniture company. He asked me to write to you and sends his regards as well.

I myself live at the Grand Hotel here, not quite as glorious as it sounds. Together with local company, I intend to weave baskets here in order to try to provide food for my family and myself.

How did you like Mr. Otto? Did he do anything for you? And have you found a good job?

Mail reaches me best via my brother's address: 46 Regent Road, Leicester.

Please send my best to your parents in this circuitous manner.

And to you my warmest regards,
Stefan Pauson

———

In England, Pauson had hoped to establish himself in Wiggan's basket-making trade. It had all been carefully planned. When seeking a way out of Germany, he had asked a fellow basket merchant in Wiggan for assistance. The British merchant complied, writing a letter stating that Pauson, due to his expertise and experience, would join his business as a partner. "The British were not willing to take Jews who would take employment away from their own people," explains Pauson's daughter. "Consequently, you had to be able to state that you were going to manufacture and create employment and not take it away."[7] Eva believes that the merchant's letter was crucial to her parents' emigration.

When he arrived at the Wiggan plant, eager to start work, Pauson was stunned to learn that the business was suffering a downturn. There were no plans to expand, to add a new partner, or even to have Pauson enter the business as an employee. The British manufacturer explained that his letter had merely been a ruse to help Pauson escape Nazi Germany. "My father went frantic," Eva remembers. "He was beside himself. And as young as I was, I said, 'But Dad he helped to get us out, be glad.'"[8]

In time, Stefan Pauson would regain his resolve and manage to beat back the problems that arose, as would his friend in America, Luzie Hatch.

6

Looking
Back Home

Luzie's first three months in the United States had been filled
with tumult, tension, and challenges. Yet she had done well. She
had secured affidavits for her family and for her uncle Salomon,
incarcerated in a concentration camp. Although her hope of reentering the merchandising world had not been realized, she had
secured a temporary job at the American Jewish Committee as
a special project assistant. In addition, she had averted a potential
breach with her cousin Arnold.

These were not insignificant achievements, and they had been
accomplished while she was learning her way around the expansive
New York City subway and bus routes, becoming adjusted to the

climate and new foods and sharpening her English. What was unusual and strange was beginning to become comprehensible.

Yet there was an element of New York life that would remain shocking—the American attitude toward events in Nazi Germany. As a guest at a Jewish event held at one of the city's more elegant hotels, it had not been the lavish food, the beautiful dresses, décor, or the music that had impressed Luzie. Standing at the edge of the room, looking out at the attendees, she could only think, "Don't these people have *any* idea what is going on in the world?"

As a German Jewish refugee, Luzie knew all too well what was unfolding back home in Berlin. Past experience had, of course, been the basis of her knowledge. Added to this would be information carried in dozens of letters from family members, Jewish friends, and her one non-Jewish correspondent, a former work colleague identified only as Muhme, German for "aunt." That Luzie used this term of endearment is indicative of their close relationship. Muhme's letters were not about visas, quotas, and ship tickets but rather filled with office news and gossip.

Many years later, in an intimate conversation with an AJC staffer, an event that was rare for Luzie, she revealed that she had had a "beautiful life in Berlin." Certainly an important element of that life had been her prized position at L. S. Mayer. Understandably, she maintained a keen interest in the firm's fate.

Under Nazi rule, there were only two possible fates for Jewish-owned businesses such as L. S. Mayer. Thousands went bankrupt as a result of boycotts by customers and suppliers, the smashing or smearing of store windows, and vicious threats. Businesses that escaped bankruptcy, no small feat, faced Aryanization: they were "transferred" to Aryan ownership. Technically, the Jewish owner was not robbed of his property but sold it to an Aryan. Yet these sales were far from normal business transactions; threatened and bullied, fearing for his life and that of his family and anxious to leave Germany, the Jewish businessman often came to the table and signed away his business for a sliver of its worth.

A scathing description of the process was left behind by a bold Aryanization consultant in his letter of resignation:

> I refuse to be involved in any way with Aryanization, even though this means losing a handsome consultancy fee ... I [can] no longer stand idly by and countenance the way many Aryan businessmen, entrepreneurs and the like ... are shamelessly attempting to grab up Jewish shops and factories etc. ... as cheaply as possible and for a ludicrous price. These people are like vultures, swarming down with bleary eyes, their tongues hanging out with greed, to feed upon the Jewish carcass.[1]

The first and most obvious result of this nationwide fire sale on Jewish establishments was that Jewish entrepreneurs were stripped of their finances. But this disaster was more than financial. A business is often about more than making a living—it becomes part of the owner's personality and identity—and, for people like L. S. Mayer, Luzie's employer, part of a long family tradition.

The enterprise had begun as a dry goods company founded by Loeb Solomon Mayer in Frankfurt in 1822. Mayer enjoyed great success, in no small measure due to his wife, Betty, as noted in the company's centennial booklet.

> Mrs. Betty developed a great ability in business matters and proved to be a dynamic entrepreneur, even though the notion of women's emancipation was foreign to her. She

ran the business independently after her husband's death and traveled regularly to the Leipzig Trade Fair. In an era when all traveling was done by stagecoach, this was a considerable accomplishment for a woman.[2]

While Loeb and Betty Mayer laid the company's foundation, it was their grandson, Leo S. Mayer, who sparked the firm's remarkable growth. The company would expand well beyond Frankfurt with the opening of offices in Pforzheim, Berlin, Paris, and New York. There was also an L. S. Mayer, Ltd., of London, which, though technically a separate company, was in many ways integrated with the German division.

A 1930 auditor's report described L. S. Mayer as a "leading, well respected export business," with annual sales exceeding ten million reichsmarks.[3] The company had 158 employees, in addition to 34 apprentices and 74 industrial workers. Luzie joined this prestigious firm in 1933 as an assistant to a top executive.

Luzie's correspondence is replete with affection for the firm and her work there, as well as her hopes of one day reentering the business world. What about L. S. Mayer so appealed to this young woman?

L. S. Mayer did not function as a typical middleman between factory and consumer, purchasing open market goods available to all and reselling them; instead, the company often designed and patented its own goods.[4] This creative element certainly could have been attractive to Luzie.

A shopper sees a finished product, such as a leather handbag, on a store shelf. Delighted with it, she buys it, never knowing all the detailed work that went into its design and production. But Luzie knew this behind-the-scenes process well. She saw and was perhaps at times part of the discussions about a sample's fine points. Was the bag's closure too small, the handle large enough? Was the leather dull, the color slightly off? The journeys from idea to sample and then from sample to approved design likely added interest to her job.

Luzie worked at L. S. Mayer until her exit from Berlin in October 1938. In this she was fortunate, for by 1938, approximately 70 percent of Jewish-owned businesses in existence when the Nazis assumed power had either failed or been Aryanized.[5]

How had L. S. Mayer survived the first five turbulent years of Nazi rule? The answer can be found in the *White Book*, a multivolume chronicle of the Nazi Germany's anti-Semitic policies from 1933 to 1939, sponsored by the American Jewish Committee.[6] Luzie was a project assistant on the *White Book*. She likely typed the manuscript and helped compile and translate the cited material. The *White Book* draws on a wide range of sources, including Nazi legislation, government circulars, newspapers, posters, and leaflets. Also cited are German-Jewish documents: newspapers, journals, and reports from community organizations. Nothing within the AJC Archives identifies those in Germany who were forwarding the information to the AJC in New York. Yet we do know that the project, at least when Luzie worked on it, was directed by a woman named Margarete Muehsam-Edelheim, former editor of the *C. V. Zeitung,* one of German Jewry's chief newspapers. The *White Book* encompasses the full scope of Jewish life in Germany: the civil service, education, army, agriculture, special tax regulations, registration of Jewish property, and many other subjects.

Within these volumes there is much that touches on, and explains, L. S. Mayer's fate. It is essential to remember that L. S. Mayer was not part of the retail world but part of a universe that existed in the background—the wholesale sector. The company's Berlin office at the corner of Ritterstrasse had nowhere near the foot traffic of a store on the Kurfürstendamm, the city's elegant shopping boulevard. L. S. Mayer didn't need the thousands of clients that traipsed into a large department store, for their clients, though fewer in number, bought in bulk. Although L. S. Mayer made a grand statement, with its large signs and corner location at Ritterstrasse, this was hardly the case for all wholesalers. Unlike a retailer, a wholesaler can be located on a third or fourth floor of an office building, out of sight to casual passersby.

Their less prominent locations helped the wholesale businesses survive since the Nazis needed to be stationed at prominent spots to spread their vicious propaganda. "The wholesale trade," the *White Book* explains, "does not furnish such a good object of attack for propaganda purposes because it is not as visible to the man in the street, as the retail store with its manifold displays."[7]

There was also the important issue of capital. An Aryan interested in buying a Jewish business needed far less capital for a bakery or a shoe store than for a large enterprise with multiple locations, such as L. S. Mayer. Furthermore, as the *White Book* notes, managing a store, though not easy, certainly lacked the complexity of a wholesale operation. "It is much more difficult to replace quickly the special market experience of a wholesaler. Therefore the rough methods of political warfare were avoided in the case of the Jewish wholesale trader in favor of the slower method of economic exclusion."[8]

Finally, L. S. Mayer was more than a domestic wholesaler; it was also an exporter. The Nazis did not immediately turn on Jewish export companies that had foreign connections and brought hard currency into Germany. Thus, Jewish export firms were treated at first with greater caution than other Jewish firms.

So Luzie's employer had survived into 1938. But surviving and prospering are not the same. In 1931, the company had sales exceeding ten million reichsmarks; in 1938, the sales had slipped to two million reichsmarks.[9]

The bad news continued. In the summer of 1938, a significant tax penalty was levied against L. S. Mayer for the alleged violation of customs regulations. It is impossible to know whether the fine was for a legitimate violation or was merely a Nazi ruse to "legally" extract money from a Jewish firm. At the time, Jewish companies were under assault for one violation after the next, from tax infractions to the breaking of "hygiene" laws. In any event, L. S. Mayer went ahead and paid the penalty, for what choice was there? Any protest of innocence would have risked the possibility of fierce Nazi retribution.

The firm, after all, was being watched. The L. S. Mayer surveillance file, maintained at the Frankfurt Chamber of Commerce, was growing month by month. In June 1938, a staffer recorded that "conditions within this Jewish company are rather murky. We heard that the Jew Nachmann has a bad reputation among Aryan employees due to his Jewish audaciousness."[10]

L. S. Mayer, which had existed in Germany for more than a hundred years by following the motto "Always Evolve," was, by the time of Luzie's departure, facing a precarious future.

Hired years before Luzie, Muhme had been one of Luzie's closest friends at L. S. Mayer. Although details are unknown, during Kristallnacht Muhme had more than proved her friendship and had been of great assistance to both Luzie and her father. As an Aryan she had been able to stay on at L. S. Mayer, and she kept Luzie abreast of all that was changing.

———

To: Luzie Hatch, New York
From: Muhme, Berlin
Date: March 6, 1939
Translated from the German

Dear Miss Hecht,

From now on I will write back to you promptly, since I now have the time!!

You must surely think I am very disloyal for only now answering your letter from December of last year. In any case, I immediately got in touch with your mother and dispatched her to come and see me in the store. Naturally, I wanted to sell her much more than she needed. Despite my cajoling, she only took the things that she wanted. So of course there was nothing more that I could do.

I can just see you prancing around in our beautiful things. Now, if only you, dear Luzie, could gain a foothold there and find a position that satisfied you.

I am lacking both the desire and the time to tell you everything in detail. You cannot even imagine what has been going on here. On December 31st, we had to evacuate the premises. Only the front room, the conference room, the private conference room, and the counter in the back where Erna used to sit remained for processing. In any case, it was an amazing operation.

In Frankfurt there are two pro tempore directors and one public fiduciary. Mr. St. [Strauss][11] did not return to Frankfurt from his trip to Italy but went directly to London, where he still is today.

In the last third of January, we heard that our company would be Aryanized after all. Pf.[12] wrote to me that Mr. Rosenberg, an Aryan, was coming to Berlin with the new coworker. Since we no longer had a store and wouldn't have been able to rent one that quickly, he would showcase the merchandise in a hotel. I had to put myself at the gentlemen's disposal and invite the customers in advance.

I did that, and worked together with Mr. Rosenberg in the hotel until Feb. 13. The success was not what the gentlemen had imagined, as the timing was very unfavorable. The competition had already eaten away at some of the money; also there had just been a clearance sale and the department stores were having physical examinations. Also, they only wanted to buy from companies where the Aryanization had already been completed, even though I was able to produce a form saying that we had been approved by the chamber of commerce.

Dresdner and I each kept one suitcase and leather goods, and we continued selling out of the apartment. I had to, since I am still drawing a salary until 03/31. As of today, we have sold K 4.000 without being in the hotel. A remarkable accomplishment, no?

Miss Volbrodt, the good Erna, found a very comfortable secretarial position through Lipski. Miss Schwarz and Ida Eichler found employment in the pattern business with Rudfluwe, and Ella is a packer with Nord und Süd. I almost forgot that Mr. Berlin is a salesman with Fodry & Bartenbach Pforzheim. Only Mrs. Wünsch, Erna Ende, and I, we still have no new position. And I don't want to quit yet either. It has all been a little much for my nerves and my sick heart. Now I have to see to it that I recover, and then it can start again.

Saturday, eight days ago, your dear parents bade me farewell. Of course they will be corresponding with you. Your father was very confident. He only regrets that you are so alone over there.

Write soon, I am enclosing an international reply coupon for you.

With love from your
Muhme

———

7

Escape to Shanghai

When Muhme had said farewell to Luzie's family, she had wished them well on what would be a vast journey, a voyage to Shanghai. Seeing not refuge but squalor, danger, and confusion, Arnold remained firmly set against the family's Shanghai venture. "Mr. Hatch," Luzie wrote to a friend, "sees Shanghai like a red rag to a bull; he would rather see my parents in Germany!" Edwin Hecht, however, recognized that remaining in Berlin was the far greater danger. By this time, it would have been difficult for a German Jew to think otherwise. Kristallnacht set in motion a stream of anti-Jewish measures that robbed Jews of their property and severely restricted their freedom of movement and participation in German life.

Just two days following the pogroms, after being stricken by the horror of the destruction of their businesses and places of worship, German Jews were dealt another blow. The victims became the criminals. They learned that they were to be held financially responsible for the enormous damage of Kristallnacht. A punitive fee of one billion reichsmarks was levied on the Jewish community. In addition, despite years of paying insurance premiums, Jewish merchants were not allowed to collect insurance for their destroyed property; the state confiscated all such payments. Further, beginning on January 1, 1939, the Jewish community was to be barred from all business activity. The Jewish Telegraphic Agency noted, "Numbed by terror and despair, German Jews today received the sentence of economic death."[1]

The Nazi goal was to remove Jews not only from the nation's economic life but from all "German" life. On November 15, 1938, Jewish children still enrolled in German schools were expelled. Four days later, Jews were excluded from the general welfare system. On December 6, Jews were banned from attending cultural and sporting venues such as cinemas, theaters, skating rinks, and bathing facilities.

So in the winter of 1939, the Hecht family left for the port of last resort, Shanghai. Here was the one place in the world that did not require a visa, a health certificate, a quota number, or an affidavit for entry. Thousands of European Jews chose a similar path. Each month about two thousand refugees poured into the city of Shanghai.

Luzie's brother Ralph recalls that in preparation for the departure, his father and the German Jewish community in general "got this fantastic idea that you should have a trade." Abandoning traditional high school studies like literature and mathematics, Jews began studying practical trades in order to have a skill that would be useful, in any setting, wherever they might land. And so, toward the end of 1937, Ralph Hecht, now fourteen and a half, left the Theodor Herzl School to apprentice with a tailor.[2]

The garment-maker Ralph worked for was an Ostjude, a Jew from eastern Europe. By the mid-1920s, the Ostjuden, most of whom had immigrated in the years surrounding the Great War but some of whom had been in Germany for up to two generations, represented 25 percent of the Jewish community of Berlin, hardly an insignificant proportion. Yet for most German Jews, their east European coreligionists were a presence in the city but not in their lives. "Brothers and Strangers" is how one historian of the period has described the relationship of the two groups.[3]

German Jews, well educated and acculturated, tended to look askance at their east European brethren, who occupied lower rungs on the social and economic ladder. But regardless of what Edwin Hecht's personal feelings may have been toward the Ostjuden, he realized that here was a community with skills that could prove to be quite valuable for immigrants making their way in a new land.

Edwin had expected that his son, Ralph, would become a tailor. But Ralph readily admits that most of his time was spent cleaning "the damn shop." Nevertheless, in his six to seven months as an apprentice, he did learn the basics: how to hem a garment, put a button on a coat, and take measurements.

Even more pressing than a trade was the issue of language. Edwin Hecht hired a Mr. Weber, one of the thousands of Jewish artists banned from working in the cultural arena, as his son's private English tutor. Before the advent of Nazism, Weber had delighted in his work as a bandleader, interpreting musical pieces, leading musicians, and performing before audiences. Now Weber performed as an English teacher for Jewish clients hoping to cram in as much English as possible before leaving Germany.

He spent his days with nervous students conjugating English verbs, drilling basic requests, repeating common phrases, and reading and rereading dialogues. "Weber had been reduced to garbage. He didn't like the idea of giving lessons," Ralph recalls. "He thought it was one step below him."[4]

Despite his distaste for the work, Weber was an excellent teacher. By the time Ralph left Germany, he had acquired the basics of conversational English, a great asset in the port city of Shanghai, where English was the lingua franca. Neither Ralph nor most of the Shanghai natives he encountered on the city streets had a full command of English. Both spoke broken English, each with their respective German and Chinese accents, and yet somehow they could communicate.

The task of packing the family belongings went to Luzie's stepmother, Helene. But packing was not a solitary event—a German Nazi stood by to ensure that no valuable items were slipped into the shipping crates. In the end, a lifetime of family memories was pared down to eight crates loaded onto the *Potsdam*, a ten-thousand-ton ship bound for Shanghai.

Luzie's parents left most of their belongings, furniture, dishes, and clothing behind in Germany. Also left in Berlin were most of their cash assets. Back in 1933, when Luzie's father lost his full-time merchandising position owing to political circumstances, he had begun work as an independent sales representative. The mention of his dismissal from the Josef and Walter Dobert Company in 1938 is therefore a bit mystifying. Was Edwin Hecht still self-employed? Was Josef and Walter Dobert Company one of his many clients, or had he obtained full-time work at the firm? In any event, in May 1938, the company received this notice from the German Labor Front: "The Jew Edwin Hecht ... has to be removed immediately from his workplace. It is not acceptable anymore that the Aryan workforce has to share the same workplace as a Jew. His termination has to be reported immediately to Berlin."[5]

Luzie's father was promptly dismissed. "We would not have terminated you ourselves," his employer stated, "since we were always satisfied with your performance. Things have become quite difficult for us, too, since we don't have an agent to substitute for you."[6]

Whether he had been a Josef and Walter Dobert employee or an independent sales representative, Edwin Hecht was probably forced to dip into his savings to cover his family's daily expenses after the loss of this income. Savings were also needed to pay punitive taxes and levies, such as the Reich Flight Tax.

And there remained yet another financial obstacle. Emigrants could leave with just ten reichsmarks in cash. Any remaining funds were placed in a blocked account that could be used only for specific purposes approved by the Currency Office for Foreign Exchange in Germany. Nazi thievery masqueraded as a litany of taxes and regulations that ensured that when these unwanted Jews left, the wealth they had created would remain in Germany.

And so, when Luzie's family set sail for Shanghai, they did so with limited possessions and a paltry sum of money. They were leaving the horrors of Nazism behind, yet they encountered its vestiges during their passage. Even on a ship, plying the vast ocean waters thousands of miles from Germany, a Jewish identity still meant certain restrictions.

"Out of consideration for the Aryan passengers' well-known disposition," it was announced, Jewish passengers in tourist class were to be restricted to the smoking room on starboard. Although Jews could use the swimming pool, they could do so only at specific hours, thus ensuring that Aryans would be able to swim in a Judenrein pool.

Years later, Ralph can still remember the ship's numerous ports of call. After leaving the German port of Bremerhaven, the first stop was Rotterdam, where representatives of the city's Jewish community came aboard with a financial contribution for their German brethren. The *Potsdam* continued on, docking in Southampton, Gibraltar, Genoa, Port Said, Ceylon, Singapore, and Kobe, Japan, before finally reaching Shanghai. The Hechts were touring the world, a world closed to Jewish refugees. At each port along the way, non-Jewish travelers disembarked; by the journey's end, the passenger list was almost entirely Jewish.

As the *Potsdam* neared the Chinese coast, passengers on deck peering anxiously for a glimpse of their new home could hear the sounds of the port: "Hay! Oho! Hay! Hayhay!" "Such is the yell that first strikes the ears of the new arrival at Shanghai," wrote a diplomat stationed in Shanghai. "It is a hungry yell, a pleading yell, a wild yell such as only the throat of a Chinese coolie can emit."[7]

The piercing call of the dockworkers was an announcement that Luzie's family and the other refugees had arrived in an unfamiliar and new world that would be their temporary home. "It was," recalled one German refugee, "different than anything you ever could have imagined. Nothing could have prepared us for what we saw. Nothing."[8]

For Ernest G. Heppner, a seventeen-year-old from Breslau and fellow passenger on the *Potsdam,* it was one of the city's daily routines that jarred: "Every morning coolies pushed carts around the city to gather up, depending on the weather, sixty to eighty corpses from the streets. I was particularly disturbed to see the bodies of many babies and children ... These were often baby girls whose parents either did not want them or could not feed them and lacked the money for a funeral."[9]

Shanghai was a densely packed city on overload. Its narrow, jammed tangle of alleys and lanes had nothing in common with the pristine, neatly planned avenues of Berlin, where pedestrians moved in orderly fashion. Encounters with the city's armies of beggars were described repeatedly by Western visitors. An American journalist noted:

> Slowly you moved on, not quite certain whether you were the one who pushed or who was being pushed. Hemmed in by the ten thousand blank and hairless faces ... you were wondering. But the ten thousand were not wondering. Not a bit. No one would give you so much as a look.
>
> Except the beggars. Horribly disfigured people would stretch their rotting limbs toward you. Half-starved mothers would hold up their half-starved babies.... Old men would follow you for two or three blocks, murmuring pleas in the first block, obscenities in the second, curses in the third. And you were wise to drop your dragon coppers into their hollow hands. You did not know, of course, that in the fourth block they were likely to transfer some of their lice to your coat. You did not know that begging, as every other racket in this wide-open town, was an organized monopoly.[10]

German Jews, members of their nation's middle and upper middle classes who had lived in decent apartments and houses, now moved into small rooms and apartments located off narrow, dirty, dark alleys. Families often shared their crowded, meager living spaces with other refugees.

Edwin Hecht was fortunate to find an apartment with plumbing, but others were not so lucky. For some, their toilet was a "honey pot," a bucket. Each morning, slowly weaving their way through the Shanghai streets, were the honey pot collection wagons that gathered the previous day's human waste. The wagons' pungent contents were transported to outlying farm areas for use as fertilizer. Not surprisingly, fruits and vegetables had to be washed with a special soap. Even rice, a Chinese staple, required an extra step before cooking. From the bag it was poured onto a plate to jostle the bugs nestled within. Once the rice settled, the insects would scurry to the surface, where they could be removed.

The poor sanitation, poverty, overcrowding, extreme weather, and lack of medicine bred a kaleidoscope of diseases: scarlet fever, typhoid, dysentery, cholera, and others. In the area known as the International Settlement, the section of Shanghai that would be home for Jewish refugees from Germany, in one year alone, 1937, more than twenty thousand corpses were collected off the streets.[11]

Yet for all of its drawbacks, Shanghai had historically been a blessing for many since it was an open city, with no visa needed for entry. Thousands of White Russians had fled there after the Russian revolution, and now in the 1930s, it became a refuge for German and Austrian Jews. But what was a blessing for political and religious refugees was a lure for criminals, hucksters, gamblers, adventurers, and spies who flocked to Shanghai in large numbers. It was said that the best pickpockets in the world were found in Shanghai.

As a trade port, Shanghai was an inviting target for foreign powers. Although China was a great nation with a rich heritage, its lack of financial wealth, technology, and a strong military had enabled foreign powers to carve out pieces of the city. The British, French, Americans, and Germans had all helped themselves; more recently, since the outbreak of the Second Sino-Japanese War in July 1937, the Japanese had arrived. Large areas of Shanghai, including Hong Kew, where most German Jewish refugees would live, had come under Japanese control.

Arriving in Hong Kew, the refugees found that Japanese bombings and the subsequent scorched-earth policy of the retreating Chinese army had left the sector badly scarred, with sections partially or completely destroyed. Yet, as historian David Kranzler has acknowledged, "Whatever the disadvantages, Hong Kew satisfied the two major needs of the refugees, low rents and cheap food."[12]

The Japanese did not interfere at first with the work of European and American relief agencies. "Welcome to Shanghai. Now you are no longer Germans, Austrians, Czechs or Roumanians. Now you are only Jews," was one relief worker's welcome to the refugees. "The Jews of the whole world have prepared a home for you."[13] Indeed, a number of Jewish agencies worked hard to do as much as they could with the funds they had, which were never enough.

The first stop for arriving refugees was a processing center, followed by registration at one of the six large *heimes,* refugee centers where they could find short-term room and board, until they could find lodgings in Shanghai. Arriving at the heime, refugees had a chance to catch their breath and get their bearings.

With the exception of one heime, all sleeping quarters were dormitory style, with the men being separated from the women. With limited storage space, most refugees lived out of their suitcases. Many possessions brought from Germany soon succumbed to the mold and mildew of the damp climate.

Established in August 1938, the International Committee for Granting Relief to Europeans (IC) offered important legal and financial services. Acting as a banking service, the IC accepted deposits and cashed the checks that the refugees had received from friends and family overseas. If an immigrant needed to convert valuables into cash, the IC Thrift Shop assisted. In addition, the IC administered a Rehabilitation Fund, providing resources for refugees to open businesses and establish a modicum of economic independence.

In time, the German Jewish refugees would rebuild the parts of Hong Kew that had been pounded during the Sino-Japanese War, opening German-style cafés, restaurants, and shops. They would create their own cultural and recreational world, establishing music and acting groups, sports clubs, and newspapers. These were impressive accomplishments. After all, the refugees had been forced from their homeland, robbed of their property, even incarcerated in concentration camps. They were now coping with a world that stood in stark contrast to their western European homeland. And it was not just thoughts about everyday survival in Shanghai that consumed them; constant worries about those left behind certainly took a toll. And yet misery and worry did not overtake them, and for this they deserve great credit. So, too, the other side of the coin is the work of the relief agencies. The magnitude of what they achieved is movingly summed up by a fellow refugee, Ernest Heppner, who commented on the corpses collected from Shanghai's streets: "Seeing those frozen corpses, we came to the frightening realization that we were totally dependent on the Jewish relief agencies for food and shelter."[14] Thus, even as we note the resiliency and energy of the German Jewish refugee community, we must recognize that the tireless work of Jewish relief agencies allowed these refugees to survive and even create a taste of home in Shanghai.[15]

As Luzie's family was on their voyage to this new world of Shanghai, she finally found regular employment. In March 1939, she started her job at the American Jewish Committee. This success would normally have been cause for celebration, but in her early months in New York, it seemed as though good news was never something that could be savored for long, before bad news would arrive.

Just days after accepting her job, word came from Edwin Hecht that the family might not be able to get into the International Settlement of Shanghai and would be forced to live in Greater Shanghai, the Chinese section. The news must have chilled Luzie with fear; all the Jewish relief agencies, European hospitals, banks, and other services were in the International Sector. Working at the AJC, where she had access to news from Shanghai, she would have understood that a German Jewish family had little chance of survival outside the International Settlement.

———

To: Arnold Hatch, Albany, New York
From: Luzie Hatch, New York
Date: March 6, 1939

Dear Cousin Arnold:

Today I have to report to you good as well as bad news. Let me start with the good ones:

You know I did everything to get a position and just when I came near to despair, I succeeded in finding a job with an American Jewish Committee through a recommendation of good friends. Although it is supposed to be a temporary employ for some special work, which however might last several weeks, I got the impression that there might be a chance for me to stay there even longer. I earn $20.00 a week and have to work 5 days only.

Today I received a card from the boat *Potsdam* informing me that they with Rolf, are on the way to Shanghai. I agree with you that Shanghai may be a bad place, but after all what I have heard recently, my parents and Rolf may be glad to be out of that hell over there, and I think they are envied by all remaining Jews.

My father wrote me that they will not be allowed to get into the European part of Shanghai (the only possible part of the town Europeans can live) unless they show when landing $100.00 per person. Otherwise, they would have to stay in the Chinatown and will never be admitted to get into the European section. To help my parents, I beg to ask you to send immediately by cable those $300.00 to a reliable bank of Shanghai, or the port authorities.

I am begging you for this because I don't see any other way out. I shall try to refund $10.00 per month to you. I would be only too glad if you could agree and help my parents at once.

With much love to you all,

Your cousin

Luzie

———

December 1938–August 1939

——

Arnold acted immediately on receiving her request and wrote to his bank.

———

To: Mr. Addison Keim, First Trust Company of Albany
Albany, New York
From: Arnold Hatch, Albany, New York
Date: March 10, 1939

Dear Mr. Keim:

Following our phone conversation of this morning in which you read me the letter from the National City Bank of New York, I herewith request you to go ahead with this thing by cable as quickly and as carefully as possible. Obviously, the greatest care must be used in matters of this kind because actually they are life-and-death matters for the unfortunates landing or trying to land in Shanghai.

Now, the names of the three people in question are as follows:

Mr. Edwin Hecht,

Mrs. Helene Hecht,

Mr. Rolf Hecht,

who are respectively husband, wife, and son. They were all residents of Berlin, Germany, and apparently have been able to pay their passage to Shanghai, and undoubtedly are in possession of the necessary immigration and transmigration permits. The money required, $100.00 for each one of the foregoing, is apparently some sort of a guarantee that they will not become public charges.

I certainly appreciate the cooperation of your bank and

the National City Bank in handling this transaction, and herewith instruct you to deduct the total cost of $312.00 from my personal account in your bank.

Yours very truly,
Arnold Hatch

―――

Reassured that Arnold had forwarded the necessary funds to Shanghai, Luzie could do little more but wait for news of her family's arrival. Here was a brief respite that allowed her to catch up on correspondence. One of the first to hear from Luzie was her dear colleague Muhme.

―――

To: Muhme, Berlin
From: Luzie Hatch, New York
Date: April 6, 1939
Translated from the German

My dear Muhme,

Hopefully the *Queen Mary* will be well behaved and hightail it across the ocean to deliver my most heartfelt wishes to you on your birthday. Even though I can no longer spend this birthday together with you, I am thinking of you from far away on this day. And you never know, maybe one day we will celebrate your birthday together again.

By the way, what about the World's Fair that is being mounted so extravagantly? Does it not tempt you? Granted, the crossing is a bit wobbly, as water obviously has no [wood] beams. But once you arrive here, you forget the seasickness quite soon (which can drive a person to despair when it has you in its grip, as in my case), all the more so when one has had as devastating a journey as I was "privileged" to experience.

At first I thought that I would never, ever be able to orient myself amid the turbulence of this city—even though I'm not exactly from a small town myself. But in the meantime I have adapted splendidly. I barely need to inquire about streets anymore, because the arrangement of the streets is inherently very concise. And after overcoming the initial difficulties, orienting myself became very simple and easy. So you see, now you already have an old "New Yorker" in front of you, who will be at your side anytime with advice and assistance.

I still have no word of my parents' arrival, but I very much hope that they have landed safely. Although I am not exactly overjoyed to know that they are there, nevertheless I am relieved that they have made a decision. I have a great yearning for my dear Papa, and I wish and hope to see him here in a year's time.

Your dear note for which I thank you many times made me very happy. I also wanted to tell you that I have now finally found a very comfortable position and also earn a good salary, considering the circumstances. Actually I was only hired for a special project, but I very much hope that I can stay after it ends.

If not, I can still fall into despair and hang my head. But you know that it's not that easy to bring me down. And here, too, I always try to appear cheery and fun on the outside—but what it looks like on the inside is nobody's business.

I would be terribly glad to go back to working in the jewelry and gallantry [personal care goods] business, and have already interviewed with several large companies. But the season is over now; maybe I will have more luck in the fall. You cannot imagine how well-developed the jewelry business is here. The cheap and midpriced items sell in formidable quantities—that would be something for you.

As my oh-so-modest means don't offer me the luxury of corresponding with everyone (incidentally many thanks for the answer coupon, but I would write to you anyway!), may I ask you to send my regards to anyone who has asked about me.

Incidentally, thank you so much for taking such good care of my mother.

Since the *Queen Mary* won't wait, I have to say goodbye to you for today. Next time I will tell you more about the American lifestyle and its quirks . . . —In case Dresd. has gotten married in the meantime, congratulations to him.—And to you, heartfelt wishes for your birthday—and a kiss from your

Luzie

Luzie also owed a letter to her friend in England, Arnold Godschalk. His letter of April 7 stating that he could be of no assistance in getting Luzie's family to England could hardly have been unexpected. Still, she had written him, as she had to a number of business associates, even those who were fairly recent acquaintances, because one needed to grab any chance, no matter how slight, hoping that maybe, just perhaps, a door would open.

That he was not able to help did not change the fact that he was a dear family friend. So, at the end of April, Luzie wrote him not for help but to update him on her family and share her rush of impressions about life in America.

———

To: Arnold Godschalk, London
From: Luzie Hatch, New York
Date: April 24, 1939

Dear Arnold,

I was really very happy to receive your letter of February 7th. I hope and wish with all my heart that your successes in business are growing daily and by the hour—which I couldn't expect otherwise, considering your capabilities.

Surely life in England must be nice and wonderful, especially now again, since the danger of war seems to have been averted for the time being. According to the local newspapers, it seemed as if war was inescapable. Many columns were devoted to the events in Europe, and everything was painted in the bleakest of colors.

If one didn't have so many relatives and friends there, one might—as frivolous as this may sound—endorse this solution, so that finally a change might come about. It certainly can't get any worse for us. If it should come to a world conflict, hopefully the democracies will carry home the victory.

I have had the good fortune to find a position with a

committee [American Jewish Committee]. The work interests me a lot, we are treated well, and I only hope that after completion of this special project—which is all that I was actually hired for—I can also stay on. At the moment I am Dr. Edelheim's secretary, the former editor of the *C.V.*-newspaper, who also knows Grete Carpus well (her name happened to come up in conversation). It is such a small world after all.

I only have to work five days and therefore on Saturday/Sunday I can recover from the strain of the week. You know that I am no "country girl," but that is how I felt during my first few weeks here. The formidable pace, the many people, the vast number of cars, all of this impressed me so much that I thought that I would never find my way around.

Of course all that quickly subsided, and now I whiz around by subway—the only available means of transportation if one wants to get anywhere at all—like a native New Yorker through the giant metropolis with its great distances. Even the many Negroes (here one has to say "colored people"!) don't stand out anymore. Still, the American is very different from us, more than I previously thought. One must also adjust to his mindset so as not to stand out as a "refugee."

New York is an interesting city, full of contrasts. The most marvelous, grandiose houses—next to them the ugliest, smallest houses. The newest, most elegant cars drive next to the oldest Fords from the year X before Christ, add to that an assortment of almost all the tribes of the earth.

The business world actually interests me a lot in general, and if I am really laid off from the committee after the special project comes to an end—which I do not hope, wish or expect—then I would really like to find a position in a wholesale business, even though I would have to start off very small again and may not—although certainly after a long time—again attain the kind of position that I had at L. S. Mayer.

I am astonished myself that this letter has gotten so long, because usually I tend to make it brief, since I have such an enormous correspondence that everyone has to content themselves with scantily worded letters. So you can pride yourself on this obvious display of preferential treatment and answer me soon out of recognition.

The World's Fair opens next week, and it is supposed to be fantastic. Only people are concerned that many European visitors will be deterred due to the political situation, and therefore the event will not enjoy the anticipated level of commercial success. Wouldn't you like to see this exhibition? Maybe you will take the most brilliant ideas back to England with you. I would be awfully happy to play tour guide and initiate you into the secrets of New York life, as far as I know them.

Your already quite elderly Friend,
Luzie

P.S. This week I have taken the first step towards becoming a proper American; I have obtained the "First Papers."

———

In May, the long-awaited news from Luzie's family arrived. They had landed in Shanghai and were now safe in the city's International Settlement.

To: Luzie Hatch, New York
From: Helene Hecht, Shanghai
Date: April 1939

On account of the many new impressions I got in the last weeks it was impossible for me to write you earlier than today. Anyhow, I now am in a position to speak frankly and can write the truth. We couldn't stand it any longer in Berlin. Father as well as Rolf were always in highest danger and I would have become mad had it not come to an end. New arrests were made every day, not so many as in November, but whenever the bell rang, we were afraid that it was the police.

F. lived through terrible occurrences. In the camps the men suffered awfully. Hundreds of them have not returned home, and those who were lucky to be released were hardly to be recognized by their relatives and friends. With bald scalp and emaciated they are returning home. On one of their famous collection days we were not permitted to leave our apartments. It was disgusting when leaving the house to see all the posters and inscriptions.

Believe me that we would have waited for another way out had we had the possibility, but we couldn't stand it any longer. Whatever I am writing cannot give you the idea of what really occurred because it cannot be given in words.

The passage on the boat which we thought to be delightful was also a disappointment. Unfortunately the *"Risches"* [evil ones] weren't missing. There always were Nazis aboard who made our life disagreeable even there. We were not permitted to enter the reading room and bathing was only allowed until 3 o'clock in the afternoon. The permitted smoking room was too small, and one didn't know where to stay at bad weather.

Except the tropical heat between Suez and Hong Kong, it was always rough and cold. Under different circumstances, this trip could have been very interesting. We saw many exotic and exciting things never to be forgotten in life.

After landing at Shanghai, we received a letter from the American bank with Arnold's remittance through the representative of the North German Lloyd. I cannot describe our feelings. We were so depressed and afraid of our future in our new homeland. Now we were released, however, of the sorrows for our daily bread.

Shanghai is a very big and lively town. It swarms all around with people, mostly men. Until now 6,000 emigrants are here, and some thousands more are expected. Through the immense immigration the rents for rooms have been largely increased. We pay 60 Shanghai dollars for a very small and simply furnished room. It is situated in a fully battered suburb named Hong Kew. It is impossible for us to stay here for good, but we must take our time to look for something else. One side of the street has been rebuilt scantily by the emigrants, and small shops have been established. The other side is a deserted battlefield.

We take our meals in a refuge-home together with many hundred people. Sometimes we have to stand for hours before getting a seat. We get every noon a warm soup with some meat in it, by the way in a damaged dish with spoon, without knife and fork. We have to sit on long endless benches without back. As long as we have no income, we are going there, and though some people don't like it, in Oranienburg or Weimar, it is a thousand times worse.

We bought us a small spiritus boiler to be able to cook at least some coffee or cocoa when the meal wasn't sufficient. We do not get any financial support because the number of the immigrants is too high. In the French or the International sections it is of course much nicer, but much more expensive.

The view of the streets is peculiar. We hear mostly Chinese, but English speakers get along. We improved much in Germany, but we didn't learn long enough. The poor Chinese live in the streets. They are cooking their special dishes in oil all day, unsavory and not eatable for us Europeans. They eat while walking and standing and live in dirty house entrances. That applies only to the poor population. I am convinced that the well-to-do Chinese have at least as much culture as we have. The Chinese are utmost polite and devoted. As far as I can judge in this short time, a good business could be made after the war is over. But one has to reduce one's standard of life to a minimum for a very long time. We have to have patience and to wait to see how it might be in the future.

———

Ralph added his own letter.

———

Now I am no longer on the ship, but in Hong Kew, a suburb of Shanghai occupied by the Japanese. One believes to be in the movies going between all those battered houses. Every bridge is occupied by Japanese and military automobiles are always running through the streets. Sometimes some people are shot in the night. For this reason it is not advisable to go into the street late in the evening. Hong Kew is a very nice part of Shanghai. Formerly it was the American section. It is situated very airy and sound. In former times, all Europeans of the settlement came here for recreation.

Leaving the boat we were shocked, but one gets accustomed to everything. The eating in the *Hilfsverein* [German Jewish Aid Society] is not good but better than nothing. The emigrants are mostly very active and have already opened up many shops. I happened to have chances to get a position and hope to succeed.

Rolf

———

8

A Widening Circle

With her immediate family out of Berlin, Luzie could turn her attention to other family members. Among those looking for an exit from Germany was Aunt Paula Steinberg, the sister of Luzie's deceased mother, Johanna. Her children, Erna, Walter, and Hilde, had emigrated to Palestine, leaving Paula quite alone. In her letter, Luzie apologizes to her aunt, who was angry at her for not writing sooner, and she shares with her what life in New York was like.

To: Paula Steinberg, Dortmund, Germany
From: Luzie Hatch, New York
Date: May 1, 1939
Translated from the German

My dear, beloved Aunt Paula!

I heard from my father that you are very angry with me, which on the one hand I can completely empathize with. On the other hand, I hope that after reading this letter, you will have found a little understanding for me and for my silence.

After all the initial turmoil, I have finally come into my own somewhat and am beginning to lead an ordered life, so that from now on—I give you my word of honor—I will be in touch with you regularly.

Before I tell you about myself, I would like to enquire about you. First of all, how is your health? When can you start thinking about achieving your plans? If there is any way that I can be helpful and obliging to you, I beg you with all my heart to let me know immediately. You know that I will do my utmost and take care of everything I possibly can. Now, it is not at all clear to me to what extent your ideas can be accomplished—perhaps you would be interested in coming here at some point. Although these prospects are also very bleak, perhaps we should try to see if there are any possibilities—of course always under the assumption that everything else works out. Please share your views on this with me.

Aunt Martha married again three weeks ago; she needed some support. I hope that she chose the right man. I hear very little from all the other relatives. I also haven't written to anyone so far, because it has been absolutely impossible for me.

The crossing took a big toll on me. I was constantly seasick, and after my arrival I felt like the hotel where I spent the first night was rocking back and forth. My cousin once removed (my father's cousin) picked me up, along with several old friends who have been here for a while.

My cousin is a very kind man, a typical American. He does not speak a word of German, and I was just happy that I had no difficulties in communicating right from the start. Generally I understood almost everyone right away, and was myself able to communicate quite well. In the meantime, of course, my English is making progress every day, and I have already learned a lot of new things.

The day after my arrival, my cousin drove back to the city where he lives (approximately two hours from here). Now, I am really no country girl, but at first I was so disoriented by the incredible commotion that I thought I would never find my way, to the point that I fell into desperation.

Besides, I had such a dreadfully bad room that I was also very sad about that. I was at a loss. If my best friend, who is also here, and an old colleague hadn't taken pity on me, I don't know what I would have done.

First off, they arranged for me to get a reasonably nice room. I rented it for only a few weeks because it was too expensive. And then finally I moved for the third time. I went to my cousin Edith's house—Aunt Martha's married stepdaughter, who arrived four weeks before me. I feel very comfortable with her. I eat at her place every so often. It tastes better than a restaurant and she charges me a low rate for meals.

Of course, all of this sounds a lot easier than it really was. First of all, it took weeks before I could finally unpack my things and have some peace and quiet. Then, the change in climate was so strenuous that I was constantly incredibly sleepy. I could never get enough sleep, and yet I was always tired. The weather here changes with an abruptness that is indescribable. For that reason, the climate is so taxing that it takes everyone a certain amount of time to get used to— some people never acclimate to it.

After the first two weeks I went to look for employment, and was running around in the city all day. Berlin is a big metropolis and has enough commotion, but nevertheless, nothing there was nearly as strenuous as here. The distances are much farther, and day in and day out there is such an entanglement of people—that alone is enough to befuddle you. The only way to get anywhere is by subway; it takes an eternity to reach your destination with any other mode of transportation. Many car owners don't even use their cars in the city because it takes so long to get anywhere.

The big department stores are fantastically decorated, and in general there are the most wonderful stores here. Every day the skyscrapers impress you anew and offer a different view for every type of weather. Thousands of people work in these gigantic buildings, sometimes more than the entire population of a midsized city. There are an enormous number of cinemas, and all seat a vast number of people. Most of them play all day long; there are always two films.

A Widening Circle

—

In the middle of the city is a wonderful park that stretches out for hours. There are little lakes that you can take a rowboat out on in the summer, and in the winter you go ice-skating . . . Bridle paths, big playgrounds, restaurants, etc. Apart from Central Park, as it is called, there are other wonderful parks in every corner, so that sometimes one barely has the feeling of being in this mammoth metropolis. Meanwhile, when you go into the business district—which I crisscrossed back to front during my job search—you are astounded at the scale and the large number of businesses.

Despite many good recommendations, I could only find temporary work every once in a while for the first few weeks. Every evening I would come home exhausted from all the running around and totally depressed if once again I had not succeeded. Finally now, just when I bitterly needed it, I have managed to find a job in an office. I have only been hired for a few months on a special project, but hope that I will be kept on after it ends. My supervisors and my colleagues are all very well educated and nice, which makes working together much easier.

Nicest is that I only need to work five days, and then I can always take a nice rest Saturday and Sunday. The first weeks I spent these two days off almost only in bed, because I was so exhausted. But now my body has slowly adapted to the new way of life, and I feel much fresher, so fresh that I am actually happy to be able to chat with you at length after such a long time.

Now it is beginning to be spring; the temperature is tolerable. In a few weeks it's supposed to get so hot—as happens every year—that moving anywhere is exhausting.

December 1938–August 1939
—

And due to the high level of humidity in the air, you are perpetually drenched in sweat. Now . . . we must wait for what is to come. This time will also pass, as everything does.

I am now almost 27 years old—most of these years were not too joyful. Let's hope that some more pleasant ones will follow. For the time being, it doesn't seem that way; my head is still too full with so many worries.

Let me know as soon as possible how you are doing. I am so interested to hear.

Best, best wishes and lots and lots of love and kisses

from your

Luzie

———

———

To: Luzie Hatch, New York
From: Paula Steinberg, Dortmund, Germany
Date: May 10, 1939
Translated from the German

My dear Lützken!

Your letter arrived approximately one hour ago, and you will receive an answer right away! You certainly don't deserve it, because dear Luzie, you can believe me, never in my life have I been as disappointed as I was that you couldn't write to me sooner than half a year later. I couldn't and didn't want to believe that you could be so disloyal. It really hurt me, but in the end I had to accept it.

There are no excuses. A short card while in transit or upon arrival would have sufficed to make your aunt happy. And that is also why, when your father sent me greetings from you and apologized on your behalf, I wrote to him that I no longer attach great importance to your correspondence.

It is also two months now since Erna and Gustav [Paula's daughter and son-in-law] arrived in Palestine with the children and so you can imagine my loneliness. They are living in Haifa—Achusa Maon L'Olim for the time being. Maon L'Olim is an immigrant house. Hilde welcomed them at the port and stayed with them for a week.

But now, first to you, dear Luzie! First of all, I wish you a very, very happy birthday and all the best. Above all, stay healthy and continue to be courageous, and send us your engagement announcement to the millionaire soon. Then maybe you can have me come over, because otherwise, dear Luzie, we will surely never see each other again in this lifetime.

Your letter interested me greatly. I can imagine all the misery you have put behind you, and I am very happy that your body has adapted to the climate there. After all, you already have all sorts of trials behind you, but ultimately it strengthens both the body and the nerves. I also see that in Erna, who wasn't always the strongest either.

Yesterday Dan turned one. Erna and Gustav are living in one room in Maon L'Olim until they get to the settlement. Now they must first do *hachsharah* [agricultural training program]. You can imagine how hard they are all working to bring me there. Willi gave them a guarantee for £1,000; otherwise they would still be sitting here today. Now, as soon as they are legalized, that guarantee will be written over to me, and so I hope to get there as well.

December 1938–August 1939

—

I, too, have been living in a furnished apartment here at Kaiserstr. 14 since 02/01, as Falks sold their house and immigrated to Palestine. Unfortunately, Mr. Falk died of a heart attack before the immigration, so Mrs. F. had to travel alone with her children. All doom and tragedy that one used to only read about in novels.

I eat at a boardinghouse with Uncle Jakob and a few other friends. Also the Levis from Lünen live here with me; they too are waiting for their certificate so they can join their children in P [Palestine]. Uncle Jakob also wants to leave. While he has a high number for the U.S., he has no guarantee to go to P [Palestine]. It is very difficult for him, too. Other decisions will have to be made later.

Now dear Luzie, this will have to be enough for today. I wonder if I will hear from you soon!

With lots of love and a heartfelt birthday kiss from
Your Aunt Paula

———

A letter from Muhme showed that the situation at L. S. Mayer was continuing to deteriorate.

———

To: Luzie Hatch, New York
From: Muhme, Berlin
Date: May 5, 1939
Translated from the German

My dear Lützken!
Your kind wishes for my birthday arrived April 14th. I

was very happy because you were the only one of all the Ellesem colleagues who thought of me.

I'm sitting here in Fräulein Jepp's office, who I am replacing for a few days as she is away on business in Breslau. Since I don't have much to do, I am taking the opportunity to chat with you and to practice a little at the typewriter. As you can see for yourself, I'm still sputtering around a lot, but with time it will work out! Rome wasn't built in a day either! Unfortunately, I don't have your letter at hand, so I can't respond to everything, but that barely matters. I can tell you a good deal all the same.

I still haven't started to look around for a new position, and healthwise I'm still not ready for it, because this L.S.M. affair has worked my poor heart over quite a bit. I want to relax for a few more months and maybe see to it that I find employment by the fall. For the time being I still want to file an application with the Reich insurance company. But I can only do this after July 1st when the two-year qualifying period is over. In the meantime, I'm living off my nest egg, which will soon be all depleted if nothing more comes in.

So, now I want to tell you about the fate of the L.S.M. Company, as well as its employees. I don't know if I already told you that the company first initiated insolvency proceedings and suspended payments. The hearing was April 21st. I surely already wrote to you that we, Miss E., Miss N., Mrs. W., and Mr. B. sued the company for payment of the so-called loyalty premium; for me that represents a year's salary. For that reason we already had our second hearing on April 29th. At the latter one, the settlement trustee and business manager was also present, and notified us that the settlement proceedings fell through because the business was supposed to continue operating.

The administrative office allocated funding, and now they are looking for a buyer to run the export business. The financial statement showed that there is only 300,000 in negative equity. The dismissed employees are supposed to receive something but, of course, not as much as originally determined in the agreement. A hearing has been scheduled for tomorrow, Friday, on the premises of the Labor Front, and there they will negotiate how high the individual compensation will be. The judge at the labor court tells us there is no law for loyalty premiums and that if we receive anything, it will be thanks to the Labor Front. That's one way of seeing it! "After 42 1/2 years of service!" But there's nothing you can do! Be it as it may!

I will be happy when the L.S.M. story is taken care of and I can have my peace and quiet, because otherwise you just get upset all the time. Glaserfeld's father was requisitioned to Bolivia as a doctor, and he's taking his family along with him. But he can't leave until September 1st because all the steamboats are booked. That's some consolation!

B. Basch is also still here. I don't see any possibility for him to leave either, since unfortunately he has no one outside. I hear very little from Miss Land . . . Miss Emde also has a new position as of April 1st, I believe at a textile wholesaler in the Brüderstrasse. At the beginning, she didn't want to return after the first day. We cajoled her a little, and now she likes it quite a bit, although not as much as L.S.M.

Now, everyone is pretty much taken care of, except for

Tina and myself. Tina is very down with her heart, and in my opinion the woman can't do any hard work. It is a pity that she has the burden with her daughter. You see, dear Lützken, everyone is taken care of somehow.

I won't send out this letter yet today, but instead I will wait for the hearing at the Labor Front so that I can tell you right away how it came out.

Muhme

Just now all of us signed below are coming back from the settlement proceedings at the Labor Front. I will let them speak!

Dear Lützken!

We just read your letter, and I'm happy that you are doing reasonably well, and that you have [illegible] settled in. So I wish you much success going forward and take care, and very best regards from

Erna

Dear Lucie,

Your foster mama sends you her love . . . but I can imagine the [illegible] . . . that our little Lützken is very brave.

Filchen

Dear Luzielein [little Lucie]!

Many thanks for your kind regards, because the letter was addressed to all of us. I'm happy that you have settled in somewhat, and that you are doing well. Is someone there to mother you, my dear? So, my little dear, wishing you all the best going forward.

Luise

Dear Lucie,

I read your letter with interest and consider you a role

model. And keep your head high even when it's hard, because there's no doubt that it's much more difficult for you in the big city. With all my heart I hope that you will see your Papa again soon and that things will work out well for you otherwise. First and foremost, stay healthy and keep up your good spirits. Very, very best wishes and lots of love, your

Erna E.

Dear Luzie, I wish you all the best for your future and that you will soon become a real American. Love

[illegible]

———

Information from Shanghai was slow in arriving, a fact that Luzie needed to explain to her cousin in Albany, a successful businessman accustomed to having his questions answered promptly and his instructions carried out immediately.

———

To: Arnold Hatch, Albany, New York
From: Luzie Hatch, New York
Date: June 12, 1939

Dear Cousin Arnold:

Please accept my apologies for not having answered your letter earlier. But as I understood from your letter that I first should find out more details about the situation of my parents, I decided to wait for those informations. On the very day when I received your letter, I wrote to my parents asking them to give me full details.

Please consider that it always takes four weeks one way and another four weeks the other way, that means eight weeks, until I can have the reply. As the postage for air-mail always costs at least 70 cents, it is impossible for me to write this way. Only last week I had to send my parents an air-mail letter. I got a short card from them telling me that my father had a break-down because he doesn't dare to eat enough in order to save the money still left to them. Furthermore they informed me that there was a scarlet fever epidemic. I didn't want to frighten you with these bad news, but wanted first to have the answer to my letter.

I spoke to many persons in order to help my parents. I was lucky enough to be introduced to a physician just arrived in America after having been five years in Shanghai. He gave me three letters of introduction for my parents, one to an American family (where he thinks they at least would be invited for dinner what also would be a good help in their situation), and the two others to two physicians. I at once sent these letters by air-mail to Shanghai.

After the card I didn't have any further news from my family, so that I really don't know whether father or Rolf found some work in the meantime. As a matter of fact they were not employed when they wrote me the card.

I hope that you don't misunderstand that I didn't write you before, but I always think there are so many things you have to care for, that I really don't want to bother you with our troubles—unless there is no other way out.

I would be very happy if there will be soon an opportunity to see or at least hear you as I didn't see you now for such a long time and as I like to be in your company. Should it happen that during your next visit in New York your time will be so limited that you only could call me, I give you my telephone number of the office: Murray Hill 3–6702 Ext. 35.

What do you think about my English? Am I improving? As I work in the Committee for a German lady and as I don't have many American acquaintances, and as I live with Germans, I am sorry to confess that I don't have any occasion to speak English. It is really too bad, because I have the feeling that I don't make progress.

I am with much love,

Yours, as ever,

Luzie

———

———

To: Luzie Hatch, New York

From: Arnold Hatch, Albany, New York

Date: June 13, 1939

Dear Luzie:

I have your letter of June 12th, and of course I understood that it would take quite a few weeks for you to get a response from your parents. However, I thought that it might not have been out of place for you to acknowledge receipt of my letter written early last month and say that you would try to get me the information wanted. I still think, without meaning to be too critical, that you might have done that.

I imagine that your parents need some money, and you might let me know. If so, we shall send them some more money very promptly.

I am glad that you are well, and in my opinion your English is improving very rapidly. This last letter before me now is infinitely superior to some written earlier this year, and I am certain that with the foundation you have and your ambition to improve that you will speak and write English fluently before long. As it is, you are doing very well now.

Business has not called me to New York in many weeks, but I am due there either the latter part of this week or probably next week, and will endeavor to see you then, or at the very least talk to you over the phone.

With much love to you, and Herta, and the two *tantes* [aunts], I am

Yours, as ever,

Arnold

At the start of the summer, Luzie had the chance to write to her former business associate Stefan Pauson in England.

To: Stefan Pauson, England

From: Luzie Hatch, New York

Date: June 28, 1939

Translated from the German

Dear Mr. Pauson:

Naturally, I am happy about every piece of mail that I

receive here from old friends and acquaintances. But I have to mention in particular that your nice note of March 24th made me exceptionally happy. In my thoughts I have already answered you countless times—e.g., during my daily underground travels in the beautiful New York subway, or in the evenings before I fall asleep, exhausted from the day's "heave and toil." But (and I am embarrassed to admit this) my energy never sufficed for me to actually sit down in front of the typewriter. Because I wanted to answer you in detail—and this evening I feel fresh and rested enough to do so. And I hope that after this long outpouring . . . you won't resent my long silence.

Most of all, I am happy that you have managed to safely escape from our "pleasant" fatherland—although it was with great regret that I read that you were in Dachau until December 10th. I hope you didn't fare too badly there. Unfortunately I am very well informed about life in those hells through my current job, and congratulate anyone who doesn't have to stay there too long. That I attempted to provide assistance, to the extent that it was in my genuinely meager power, as soon as I was on the boat is self-understood. I would have given a lot to spare you those four weeks or to shorten them for you, but unfortunately one had—and still—has to watch helplessly as those beasts martyrize and torture innocent people to death.

I can only hope that you will forget all those things as quickly as possible, and that you will soon once again become the basket manufacturer in "Wiggan," and make me the head of sales for New York and the surrounding villages and make my father the chief sales agent!

Please return the greetings from your busy manager brother—I wish that he, or even better, both of you could come soon to the New York "Fair," and that I could spend as lovely an evening with you again as during the Leipzig "Fair"!

Yes, New York, that is a chapter unto itself. You know me of course, and you know after all that I am not an inexperienced little country girl—but that's exactly how I felt getting to know this giant city. At first I thought that I would never find my way in this hustle and bustle. To defend my reputation, I must quickly add that in the meantime I already no longer see anything special about life. But now I really have spoken enough about myself.

It probably isn't nice that I am also writing on the back of this sheet of paper. But since I also wanted to enclose a letter for Hella—and I would ask you to be so kind as to forward it to her—I am concerned about the excess weight, which is why I did not use a third sheet.

I also wanted to tell you that in the meantime my parents have arrived in Shanghai. Thank God my local relatives sent them money, so that at least at the beginning they had some financial support. The reports that I receive from them are so disagreeable that I don't want to burden you with that. In any case, there are virtually no job opportunities there, and I don't know how my father will manage until he is able to immigrate here.

Should you by chance happen to have some connections in Shanghai or know a few people there, I would be extremely grateful to you if you could help my father out somewhat with recommendations. He seems to be terribly

December 1938–August 1939
—

down, and I would be terribly happy for him if you could write him a few lines, in case you should find the time, so that he can see that he is not forgotten. I have the feeling that would have a good effect on him psychologically. The address is: 83 Broadway, Room 2, Shanghai—Hongkew.

As it really makes me so happy to hear from you, I hope that you will honor me with a few lines again soon.

Sending my best wishes to you and your wife (although I don't know her), I remain

Your Luzie,
born Hecht!

———

———

To: Paula Steinberg, Dortmund, Germany
From: Luzie Hatch, New York
Date: June 29, 1939
Translated from the German

My dear, beloved Aunt Paula:

As soon as I am a millionaire, I will write to you with the *Clipper* [air transport][1] that plies regularly every Saturday and brings the mail to Europe in two days. But since the cost is six times that of a standard letter, I must continue to deny myself this mode of communication for the time being.

You cannot even imagine how very happy I was at your lovely, detailed letter—and what was nicest is that your birthday wishes arrived promptly on May 19th. All the other congratulations came either earlier or later, so you take the cake!

A Widening Circle
—

How are you living actually? As comfortably and nicely as at the Falks? I still think so often of the beautiful turnip greens that you put on my plate. Are those actually cultivated in P. [Palestine] as well? If not, I will come visit you there when I finally have all the millions that I always dream of at night.

I don't know if you have already heard that the World's Fair is currently taking place in New York. Last week I was invited to attend. It is a wonderful, giant exhibit. One needs days, weeks, and months if one wants to see all the offerings properly. In the evenings, when it is all illuminated, you feel like you are in a fairy-tale paradise. I could tell you about it for hours, but I see now that the page is almost full, and my ribbon won't suffice for a third page. I hope you are satisfied with this letter and are now good to talk to me.

All the best, 10,000 greetings and kisses,

Luzie

———

———

To: Luzie Hatch, New York
From: Paula Steinberg, Dortmund, Germany
Date: July 22, 1939
Translated from the German

My dear little Luzie,

You don't need to put the *Clipper* to use, because if you always keep in touch so punctually, I will have no reason to be angry with you—and we don't want to be angry from now on.

Last week my trunk was packed and sent off [to Palestine], and will also be there soon, God willing. Now only I am missing, and that is the biggest problem because if I can't get away now, which is very doubtful, it will take me at least another year, as the Oct.–March schedule has been closed. So you see that there is little hope for me, and I don't want to go to a transitional country somewhere, because then I will feel even more lonesome.

You, dear child, have had fabulous luck in all of this. And I am very happy that you are also in good health. You know I was always very worried about that.

As for news, I can tell you that Hilde and Alex have ordered themselves a second baby. They didn't want to fall behind Erna and Gustav and felt obligated, can you believe that! Nurith will turn three next month, and is a true Palestinian child. Walter has arrived near Haifa, so he has gotten closer to Erna and Gustav.

Uncle Jakob, the poor fellow, has no idea where to go.

Now this should be enough for today again. I have been writing all day and am tired now. Hopefully you will write to me again soon. Stay healthy, and also send my love and heartfelt wishes to Edith.

I give you a kiss!
Your Aunt Paula

———

A Cousin and Counterpart

While Aunt Paula hoped to go to Palestine, Luzie's cousin Alfons's desire lay in another direction, Latin America. Alfons Isack was both Luzie's cousin and her counterpart. The two had been born weeks apart in May 1912. They also shared yet another turn of fate, a most unfortunate one. Alfons's father, a German soldier in the Great War, had died when Alfons was only five, close to the time Luzie's mother, Johanna, died. But whereas Luzie suffered the loss of one parent, Alfons would lose both. At the age of nineteen, just when he was beginning to make his way as a salesman, his mother died.

Within Luzie's correspondence there is no indication that she was aware that Alfons Isack had been among the thousands arrested during the "terrible days." His Gestapo file reveals that the police arrived at his apartment on November 11, 1938, supposedly to search for "edged weapons, thrust weapons, and firearms."[2] They found no weapons, but rather than clearing him of the charge, they deemed the search "inconclusive." Alfons was admitted to the police prison at 4:30 p.m., where he signed the following statement:

I am a Jew and a citizen of the German Reich. My father died from a battlefield injury in Süchteln/Rhein 1918. My mother died 10/15/31 in Essen. I live here, with my uncle Siegmund Isack. Since 5/2/38, I have worked for the painter Widow Wertheim ... Before that I worked as a salesman for the Karsch company in Gelsenkirchen. I do not have cash in my possession. As soon as I have sufficient money in my possession to cover travel expenses, I intend to immigrate to Colombia. I am not aware of any criminal action on my part.[3]

He spent ten days in prison before being released on November 21, 1938. Most likely, the Nazis released Alfons believing that he would make good on his promise to emigrate. Given his circumstances, it would be a difficult goal to achieve.

December 1938–August 1939
—

With one Jewish business after another folding, Alfons was forced out of the sales world and into employment on an excavation site. Whether he was working for a private company or as forced labor on a Nazi construction project is unknown. What is certain is that it would be nearly impossible for him to earn the necessary funds for passage to Colombia. Desperate for a solution, he begged Luzie to get help from Arnold.

To: Luzie Hatch, New York
From: Alfons Isack, Essen, Germany
Date: July 10, 1939
Translated from the German

Dear Luzie and dear Herta!

After many long weeks I am answering your kind letter. Many thanks for the birthday wishes. I have been working in excavation for some time now. At first it was very hard for me, but one adapts to everything.

Now I would like to ask you again, please get back in touch with dear Arnold. As of today he still has not answered me, and now I have written to him again. Dear Arnold <u>absolutely must help me</u>. If he does not, I will have no chance of ever leaving.

Of course, dear Arnold will get the money back from the Colombian bank in two years. This is only meant to serve as "Vorzeigegeld" [money required for Columbian entry permit] for the government; I will not receive any of it in my hands.

I already knew that you, dear Luzie, are living with

dear Edith and you are in good hands there. What else have you been up to?

Hoping that you will be successful in granting my request, I remain with many greetings and kisses

Your

Alfons

———

———

To: Alfons Isack, Essen, Germany

From: Luzie Hatch, New York

Date: July 31, 1939

Translated from the German

Dear Alfons,

Although it is already 11 o'clock in the evening and I am dead tired, I do not want to let the *Europa* leave tomorrow without sending news to you with her.

I was very happy to receive your letter of July 10th, the content of which I have thoroughly noted. Herta, who has left with the aunts to get some rest, spoke with Arnold on the way to the resort. I asked her immediately whether your request came up as well.

She told me that Arnold had read your letter, and that she had the feeling Arnold wanted to help. Upon learning that, I decided not to approach Arnold again. Rather, I am asking you to let me know <u>as soon as possible</u> whether you have received an answer from Albany and if so, what it was. In case you should not have heard anything, I recommend that you go ahead and contact Arnold again—but <u>only</u> in

English, since he cannot read German, and that would just create another delay.

I am just so sorry for you that you always assumed that we and the other relatives only wanted the worst for you. If you had trusted us a little more, things would surely have been better. But of course, now is not the time to discuss that; at any rate, I will do what is in my power for you. I am glad that at least you are in good health again, and I hope that it will stay that way.

Unfortunately my father in Sh. [Shanghai] is not doing so well. I have all sorts of worries about him, and unfortunately I am unable to help him at all at the moment.

It is very fortunate that I still have my job and at least earn enough that I'm not a burden on anyone. That alone is more than enough to be content with.

So, my dears, I wish you well, to the extent that it is possible, and I look forward to hearing from you more often. And from you, dear Alfons, I expect a prompt response with hopefully favorable news.

With many greetings and kisses from

Luzie

———

Family members such as Alfons Isack and Aunt Paula Steinberg were not the only ones to hear from Luzie. In the summer of 1939 she began to correspond with Hans Hirschfeld, a colleague from L. S. Mayer. They had once been quite close.

When L. S. Mayer had suddenly lost its Canadian sales representative, Hirschfeld, who was fluent in English, wasted no time in stepping forward to fill this position. As an L. S. Mayer sales representative, he set off for Canada and never returned to Germany. "He was," in the words of his wife, Florence, "one very lucky kid."

When last together in Germany, Hans and Luzie had not parted on good terms. In another time they might have remained estranged, but with all of them going through so much turmoil, there was probably a greater readiness to put such things aside. And for all the hustle and bustle, which kept Luzie quite busy, she must have still felt somewhat lonely in New York. Whatever the reason, she decided to renew their friendship.

———

To: Hans Hirschfeld, Toronto
From: Luzie Hatch, New York
Date: July 27, 1939

Dear Hirschfeld:

I happened to notice in one of my notebooks that your birthday was last week, so I am taking this opportunity to send you my somewhat belated, but nevertheless sincere, good wishes. I am able to do this because I could get your address from Mr. Silbermann[4] for whom I did some correspondence.

So far as I can remember, when we last saw each other some years ago in Frankfurt, we parted after a slight disagreement. But since I am good-natured, I am writing you—I thought it would interest you to learn that I am in America.

I left Germany during the pogrom days on November 16, 1938. Up to this time I was still employed by L. S. Mayer.

My parents went to Shanghai in February of this year. You can imagine what that means to me. Miss Dembski was very helpful to my father and to me during the terrible days in November; I am still in contact with her, and I get always very detailed letters from her.

I have had already several jobs which were not satisfactory. For the last five months I have been working in the "American Jewish Committee" as secretary to the former editor of the *C.V.-Zeitung* in Berlin. I am very glad to have this work, although I still would prefer a position in our former line.

At the end of August I get a week's vacation, and it is possible that I shall go to Canada because everybody tells me how interesting and beautiful it is. Do you think such a trip worthwhile?

What are your parents doing, and how are you? I would like to hear from you and am,

With kindest regards,

(Known to you as L. Hecht).

———

———

To: Luzie Hatch, New York

From: Hans Hirschfeld, Toronto

Date: July 29, 1939

Dear Luzie:

I was very pleased to hear from you and greatly appreciated your thoughtfulness to remember my birthday. What the hell did you have to change your name for though? Wasn't Hecht good enough for you? I looked up "Hatch" in the dictionary and found my suspicion confirmed that it means "produce young from eggs." Forget it . . .

All joking aside, I am happy for you that you are in the States. I can well imagine what it means to have your parents in Shanghai, and only hope that you will find ways and means to bring them to New York too. I know how hard it is, and that the American public is not as sympathetic and susceptible as it used to be to refugees' troubles. Yet I cross fingers that you succeed.

My parents are fortunate enough to be in England: Leeds, to be exact, since April or so. My kid brother has worked there since spring 1938 in a factory, and now they live together and are comparatively happy.

What can I tell you about me? My latest achievement is evident from this letterhead [his business, Sky-line Gifts]. I am utterly happy to live here, since this country, and this city of Toronto in particular, are swell places, quite independent of any comparisons or the so-called refugee angle.

A trip to Canada during for your vacation is a good idea. You may be sure of a cordial welcome.

With kindest regards,

Hans

———

As the summer of 1939 crept to a close, Luzie feared that her work days at the American Jewish Committee, where she had been hired to work on the *White Book*, might be nearing an end. It would have been bad enough if this loss of income affected only Luzie, but her family, stranded in Shanghai, was depending on her.

December 1938–August 1939

—

She had received a letter suggesting that she had been made a permanent member of the AJC staff only to have her heart sink the next week when she opened a letter that suggested just the opposite. Everything was uncertain.

The oppressive heat of that summer, accompanied by dreadfully high humidity, had at least one advantage: it had probably tampered her emotions a bit. Who had energy to panic? "Torrid Wave Scorches City Area; 4 Dead, 4 Prostrated" was a front page *New York Times* story. In any event, once again she needed to inform her cousin of her unfortunate circumstances.

———

To: Arnold Hatch, Albany, New York
From: Luzie Hatch, New York
Date: August 10, 1939

Dear Cousin Arnold:

I have received your letter of August 4th, for which I thank you very much.

This week brought some troubles to me. You will remember that I was engaged by the American Jewish Committee for a special work, namely to write the manuscript for a so-called White Book. I always hoped that the Committee would have another occupation for me after the completion of this job. Last Friday I get the enclosed letter according to which I believed that I now belonged to the regular staff. But this was an error.

On Monday the enclosed letter was handed over to me, which speaks for itself. I showed this letter to our office manager, who told me that he didn't know anything about it and that it was a shock for him. He spoke at once to the new Director, Mr. Newman, in my behalf.

The next day I was informed by the secretary of Mr. Newman that he wanted to let me know that they were just in the middle of the reorganization and that he couldn't make any decision before all the new plans would be worked out, but there might be a possibility to place me elsewhere. So I don't know whether I still have my job after August 31st.

Dear Arnold, please don't think that I am discouraged. Of course I would be only too glad to stay. But if that should not be possible, I have the confidence that I will be able to earn my living.

Yesterday we had the most awful day of the season. But in spite of this, I am glad to be here, because, according to the last letter I got from my parents, it must be worst in Shanghai. Father is under the supervision of a physician because he has got too many white blood corpuscles. He is being treated with liver injections.

The house they lived in has been bought by a Japanese; for this reason they have to move out and are compelled to look for another room which wouldn't be so easy.

I hope that this finds you well and not suffering from the heat.

With much love,
Yours, Luzie

———

December 1938–August 1939
—

To: Luzie Hatch, New York
From: Arnold Hatch, Albany, New York
Date: August 11, 1939

Dear Luzie:

I have your letter of August 10th, and I am very sorry indeed to learn that you have received notice of dismissal from your position. This is too bad. However, in the first place, there seems to be from what you write a chance that they might find some other place for you. In any event, I know you have plenty of courage and ability, so that you need not worry over this.

If the worst comes to the worst, and you are without a job for a few weeks, you know that I will always see that you do not come to grief or want for anything. So just keep your chin up, and if the notice of dismissal is final, look around for something else.

My family arrives home tonight after four weeks in the White Mountains, and to tell you the truth, I shall be glad to have them home again as the house is very often lonely. The heat has bothered me a lot too this summer, but one gets used to everything.

Now, let me know as it gets along toward the end of this month how things are developing about your work.

With much love, I am,

Yours, as ever,

Arnold

———

As it was, things developed quite well for Luzie. She was, in her own words, a "lucky girl." Perhaps it had been more than luck. Luzie appealed directly to AJC's general secretary Morris D. Waldman, explaining, "I denied two chances of getting an employment in other branches of business because I like to work in this organization." While acknowledging that she had been hired for a temporary project, she had believed and hoped that on its completion there would be additional work for her. Never shy, Luzie closed with a request for a meeting. "I would be very much obliged for granting me a personal interview so that you may have a personal impression of my abilities."

Whether it was good fortune or the force of her personality, within her own personal New York universe, ill fortune had been avoided. She was reinstated at the American Jewish Committee as a regular full-time employee. But for those on the Continent, as the days of summer drew to a close, catastrophe would not be averted.

December 1938–August 1939
—

PART THREE

September 1939–
October 1941

9

Desperate Appeals

At 5:45 am on September 1, as most Europeans still slept in their beds, an estimated one million German soldiers began their assault on Poland. The Nazi invasion was a concentric attack, with forces moving in from the west, north, south, and east. On September 3, two days following the invasion, honoring their treaty obligations to Poland, Great Britain and France declared war on Germany. Writing to her friend Hans Hirschfeld, Luzie shared her thoughts on these ominous events.

To: Hans Hirschfeld, Toronto
From: Luzie Hatch, New York
Date: September 12, 1939
Translated from the German

Dear Hans H. Hirschfeld,

First of all, many thanks for your letter of July 29th. I'm really happy that you have the good fortune to work for a company that seems to be along the lines of L.S.M. Congratulations to you on your achievement and success.

I hope that Canada's declaration of war won't put you in an uncomfortable situation, either professionally or personally. I still cannot believe that twenty-five years later this mass murder is happening again. As I am a little older than you, I still remember how in Aachen we used to have to rush into the basement during the air raids—the lingering fear has branded itself on my memory forever.

In principle, one should be more than happy to live so far "out of gunshot," but the concern for relatives and friends in Germany, England, or France prevents one from finding peace of mind.

I want to explain my name change to you. I don't really need to defend myself, but since I am a good-natured person, I will say that I was actually not unsatisfied with "Hecht," but since this name is (1) not very easy for Americans to pronounce, and (2) my wealthy relatives are named "Hatch," I thought it would be quite appropriate for me to use this name as well. That's the explanation.

Unfortunately, I was forced to spend my vacation in

New York, as my employment status was still uncertain, and for that reason I couldn't risk spending money.

Best regards,

Luzie

———

———

To: Luzie Hatch, New York

From: Hans Hirschfeld, Toronto

Date: September 14, 1939

Translated from the German

Dear Luzie:

Today is Rosh Hashanah, and I went to the office anyhow, as I am not very religious at the moment. And I find your letter in front of me, for which I thank you very much. What touched me most and really shocked me was the attachment with all the addresses. To this end, I must say, first of all that the warmth that speaks from all these lines is to your honor.[1]

Tears actually came to my eyes, and for a long time I haven't felt such strong homesickness for our dear, dumb, yet innocent Germans, who are now approaching the ultimate doom—unless they decide to make a dramatic about-face in the foreseeable future. What is your opinion as to the likelihood of such a revolution, and do you believe that there are even enough unsatisfied people there, and that their morale will crumble sooner or later?

Now first to your letter, from which emanates that you have already acquired something of the "cynical toughness" of the American woman. Contrary to your belief, I am not an employee of the SKY-LINE [company], but instead I, myself brought it to life, designed all the samples—mostly smoker's items to retail at $1—myself, while my partner and friend (from Munich) deals with the technical planning and the internal business. I take care of sales.

The explanation of your name change is satisfactory. I find Wertheim's name dumb and Hollywoodish. I will never change mine.

Now I must work a little more and for that reason I must conclude this letter. Please drop me a line again soon. You see that I answer promptly, which means preferential treatment.

I reciprocate your good wishes for the New Year with all my heart.

Best wishes,

Hans

———

As conditions deteriorated in Europe, anxieties heightened, pleas for assistance increased, and plans for escape, as in the case of Luzie's aunt Martha Marchand Harf, became more daring. A widow with a young child, she married Fred Harf some months after Luzie left Germany. Perhaps there was a great romance between Martha and Fred Harf, but it is also true that a Jewish widow with a twelve-year-old daughter caught in a world where difficulties and dangers were rapidly multiplying must have welcomed the support of a partner.

For almost a year and a half Luzie had boarded with Edith Friedmann, Aunt Martha's daughter from her first marriage. Edith had arrived in New York a month before Luzie, finding an apartment in Washington Heights, a neighborhood in Upper Manhattan that teemed with German refugees. The two shared living space and meals—Luzie preferred Edith's cooking to the still strange American cuisine—and their New York experiences, and no doubt they spoke of Martha's situation in Germany. Thus although they were separated by thousands of miles, Martha remained a very real presence in Luzie's life.

In October 1939 when Aunt Martha sent a plea for help, it did not go to her daughter Edith but to her niece Luzie. Martha was confident that Luzie was the one who would be able to influence Arnold.

———

To: Luzie Hatch, New York
From: Martha Harf, Cologne, Germany
Date: October 31, 1939
Translated from the German

My dear, good Lützken,

I am addressing this letter to you, my dear Luzie, because I have a very important request that I would like you to submit to our dear cousin. You, dear Luzie, seem to have decidedly more influence on our cousin than dear Edith or Theo.

So we are desperately begging you for an affidavit. And if there is no other way, then at least for Ruthilein [little Ruthi] and me first—and for my dear Fred we will just have to look elsewhere in order to obtain the affidavit for him, in which case I will do what Else and Werner Simon did.

In any case, I would not be writing to you by airmail gratuitously if it weren't so urgent for Ruth's sake. I have sent you three families in the past week, dear Edith and dear Theo, who will tell you about the situation here. There is a Jacoby family, Otto Nathan and Rosenfelder. They will tell you everything, and you will immediately take the necessary steps to make something happen.

So again, please, please, please help us. My existence cannot delay here any longer.

1,000 greetings and kisses from all of us, and especially from your loving

Martha

———

Overwhelmed by all these requests, Arnold refused to file an affidavit for Martha and Ruthie immediately, and chose to wait. Luzie thus decided to try a new tactic with Arnold, suggesting that perhaps his younger brother Stephen could take over some of the responsibilities for their relatives trapped in Germany.

———

To: Arnold Hatch, Albany, New York
From: Luzie Hatch, New York
Date: November 8, 1939

Dear Arnold:

I am so happy that according to your letter of October 30, the bank transaction to Shanghai has been completed, as I just received very bad news from my parents. My brother Rolf is very sick with typhoid fever. He has been brought to a hospital and my parents are even not allowed to visit him. You can imagine how my parents feel . . . As I learned it is a very dangerous sickness, I hope that Rolf has recovered in the meantime.

I just happened to read in our office a letter from Shanghai which I attach . . . so that you will learn more about the fate of the Jews there. Please handle this letter strictly <u>confidential</u> and return it to me at <u>once</u> . . .

We got a very desperate letter from Aunt Martha from Cologne. You can't imagine what I read every day about the situation prevailing in Germany, so that I understand her plea for help. Don't you think that perhaps Stephen could make out an affidavit for her and her very nice and clever daughter?

I am convinced that there would be no trouble in case they should succeed to get to the United States one day because Aunt Martha is very capable and would find work. Besides, I think that in case of necessity her other daughter, Mrs. Edith Friedmann, would educate her little sister together with her own child.

I am sorry that this letter does not contain satisfactory news. I hope that next time I have to report better things.

Aunt Ida is getting along fine. How are you? Do I soon have the pleasure to meet or to hear from you again?

With much love,

Luzie

———

To: Luzie Hatch, New York

From: Arnold Hatch, Albany, New York

Date: November 10, 1939

Dear Luzie:

I have just returned from New York, where I did not get an opportunity to call you up and find your letter of November 8th.

There is no use using that typical American expression "I told you so," but you know that I have always felt that this whole Shanghai venture was a big mistake, and I am afraid that time will prove it so. There is absolutely no hope of any future for people of our faith marooned in that dismal war torn country, and equally no hope of getting out of it.

I note what you say about Martha Marchand, but regardless of what I would be willing to do, there is no possibility of getting anyone out of Germany under present conditions. I, too, had a desperate card from her only the other day, so that is out of the question for the time being and certainly for the duration of this war.

I have read some small parts of the enclosed transcript [Shanghai letter from the AJC Library] which you sent me, and to be perfectly frank with you, I am not particularly impressed by it. It sounds like the outbursts of some hysterical person, and without meaning to be critical or to appear too hard-boiled, I am not interested in this kind of stuff, nor will it do any good for anyone to send it to me. It sounds more or less like professional crying to me.

September 1939–October 1941

However, you might give her my love and the same for you and Herta also.

As ever,

Arnold

———

Bolivian Refuge

Amid the pleas for help, worsening conditions in Europe, and Arnold's mounting impatience, a bit of good news muscled its way into Luzie's life in the fall of 1939. Word came that the Friedländers, her close neighbors from Berlin who had been terrified in March that their ship would be sent back to Germany, had made their way safely to Bolivia. Their journey had been long, circuitous, and nerve-racking.

The Friedländers had originally sailed from Germany en route to Uruguay. In the days before they reached Montevideo, however, a startling announcement was written on the ship's blackboard. Passengers on the *Conte Grande*, the vessel ahead of the Friedländers' ship, had been denied entrance to Uruguay on the grounds that their visas were fraudulent. Perhaps the Uruguayan government reneged on its offer of refuge, or perhaps the *Conte Grande's* passengers did have fake documents. German and Austrian Jews' desperation for escape created an opportunity for swindlers selling forged immigration papers.

"So we came to Montevideo," remembers Inge Friedländer, "and sure enough, police came on board and said, your visas are false, you have no right to enter. Everybody was hysterical crying. And of course everybody tried and tried and tried, but nobody could get off."[2]

Seeking a welcoming port, the ship traveled on to Rio de Janeiro, Buenos Aires, and Chile. At each stop, the same routine unfolded. "We were always guarded," Inge recalls, "if not in the cabins but on board. Even when we went to the toilet we had policemen there. I mean they really didn't want us there."[3]

With no recourse, the captain now set sail for Europe with his unwanted and utterly desperate Jewish passengers. "It was absolutely dreadful," Inge remembers. "I grew up fast on that trip."[4] Had the Friedländers and their fellow passengers been aware of the ultimate fate of the *Conte Grande*'s refugees, their terror might have been tempered by hope. They knew just one painful fact: Uruguayan government authorities had declared that the *Conte Grande*'s sixty-eight passengers possessed illegal papers, crushing their plans of resettling in Uruguay. But this was only the beginning of the story.

Early on, the Hilfsverein Deutschsprechender (German Immigrant Aid Society) of Buenos Aires had decided that whatever the price or conditions, the ship could not return to Germany with its passengers.[5] The cost of settling these refugees in Chile was substantial. As a relief worker explained, there had been a long list of fees to be paid:

Permission for immigration into Chile, a passing permission for disembarkation in Montevideo, permission to change to another boat in the Argentine, and the continuation of the journey to Punta Arenas [Chile] had to be obtained. The whole cost were 20,000 Argentine pesos, to which are added a guarantee of another 20,000 pesos given to the ship agents, promising that none of the passengers disembarks on the journey from Buenos Aires to Arica [Chile] . . .[6]

This one emergency action had cost the Hilfsverein the equivalent of its average monthly expenditure.[7] And the *Conte Grande* was hardly the last such problem; more ships were on the way with passengers who would also be barred from disembarking, among them the *General San Martin*, which carried the Friedländers.

When the Jewish agencies focused on the urgent situation of the *General San Martin*, they were acting from experience, having just negotiated their way around one such crisis. In fact, by the time the *General San Martin* had crossed the Atlantic to Lisbon, Portugal, the Jewish agencies, unbeknown to the desperate passengers, had once again averted disaster. As the port of Lisbon came into view, the Friedländers expected to hear the all-too-familiar declaration that they would be refused entry. Instead, representatives of the Jewish community boarded bearing agricultural visas for Bolivia.

After a nine-day stay in Lisbon, the Friedländers and their fellow passengers again set sail, this time for Arica, a small port in the Chilean desert. At Arica, Herbert Friedländer, his wife, Paula, and daughter, Inge, were finally allowed to disembark, to feel grounded after what must have seemed a never-ending sea journey. After all, they had sailed from Germany to Montevideo, Buenos Aires, Rio de Janeiro, and Chile, then over to Lisbon, and finally back to Arica, Chile.

The refugees were housed at an army base run by a commander who was said to be "decent" and cooperative. Yet his cooperation was not sparked by humanitarian feelings alone; wanting to make sure that none of these unfortunates ended up staying in Chile, he was quite willing to expedite their journey to Bolivia.[8] From Arica, the Friedländers traveled by train to Cochabamba, Bolivia. The train ride, as Inge describes it, went "up, up, up, up and again up. It was

12,000 feet above sea level. It was really straight up to heaven. It was awful because a lot of people got sick and I got sick too. I mean you were glad you were somewhere you would be permitted entrance but on the other hand it was horrible. I threw up all the way."[9]

On reaching Cochabamba, as per the stipulation of their agricultural visas, the refugees were transferred to various farm areas. However, Inge had become so violently sick from the change in elevation that her father insisted she could neither go on nor be left on her own in this new city. In the end, the authorities, worn down by his fierce persistence, bent the regulations. After weeks at sea, repeated setbacks, and the terror of being sent back to Germany, the Friedländers finally had a new home in Cochabamba.

Like Luzie's family, who had fled to Shanghai, the Friedländers had found refuge in an exotic land far removed from their European birthplace and Jewish roots. Before the rise of Nazism and the subsequent wave of Jewish refugees, fewer than two hundred Jews lived in Bolivia. From 1933 to 1941 an estimated ten thousand Jews found refuge in this impoverished nation—the vast majority, seven thousand, arriving with the Friedländers in 1939.[10]

Of Bolivia's 250,000 inhabitants in 1939, about 5 percent were of European extraction. The vast majority were of Indian heritage, many of whom lived on pennies a day. There was almost no industry other than two tin corporations, one of which was owned by a Jew, Mauricio Hochshild, who frequently stepped forward to assist his coreligionists.

These are the basic outlines of the conditions framing the Friedländers' Bolivian landscape. A strange land for a Berliner but one that had welcomed them, a place where they would do surprisingly well. Working with George Simon, a Berlin neighbor who had settled in New York, Herbert Friedländer began a small business, importing merchandise from the United States and selling it in Bolivia. Eventually more Jews would make their way to Cochabamba, and a community began to emerge. With time there would be a rabbi, a one-room synagogue, German Jewish newspapers, and a social life.

This new homeland was to provide the Friedländers with more than refuge from Nazi Germany. Not long after their arrival in Cochabamba, Inge was engaged.

Luzie, who had taken time from all her responsibilities to send Inge a letter with her best wishes, was promptly answered.

———

To: Luzie Hatch, New York
From: Inge Friedländer, Cochabamba, Bolivia
Undated
Translated from the German

My dear Luzie,

You are truly a loyal soul, writing to me immediately to congratulate me, when we really haven't written to each other in ages. I can only tell you that I am really getting a swell husband and am tremendously happy.

We met here in a delightful garden café, and went out together for the first time on New Year's Eve. After that, we met at the sports ground every Sunday and went swimming afterward, until, after a seven-week courtship, we were engaged. You must concede this comes close to your justifiably famous American pace. Our engagement was really swell except that, unfortunately, the Hechts and all the other nice people weren't there.

Desperate Appeals
—

We celebrated on Saturday evening (02/17) in the same garden café where we met. We had an awesome meal that only Mother could have topped. Afterward we danced and had lots of fun. On Sunday morning something was cooking in the Friedländer household. You can't even imagine the mountains of flowers that we received. Plus, really nice, practical gifts for the "household." Don't you dare laugh.

I was very shocked to hear that you are learning to drive. I can only wish you the best of luck. You have always been such a nice and loyal friend to us that it would be truly horrible if you died such a dreadful death.

I am really pleased with my job. I earn a good salary for my age, and I have a really nice boss whom we also see socially. He was also at my engagement party. Isn't it funny that we both work at relief organizations, since the Joint [American Jewish Joint Distribution Committee] is really the same thing, just a little bigger? And speaking of careers, I also want to tell you—which you have probably already heard from Simons—that my fiancé has a really marvelous clothing store, a delightful salon that could just as well be in any other big city. I love to go there and try on all sorts of things. He owns the salon together with his relatives. This way I am getting an adorable aunt, and an uncle who is as nice as he is funny. Auntie is all of twenty-seven years old.

We actually live quite well here. Tonight we're going to the movies to see the Dietrich film <u>Angel</u> that probably had its world premiere five years ago, but that doesn't matter. There are so many American films here, one older than the other; many of them are very good. Recently we saw the animated film <u>Snow White</u>. Hopefully you, too, will recover from your illness. Why did you have to catch such a stupid flu? I don't want to hear any more of that from you, do you understand?

Hopefully I have made everything up to you and told you everything worth knowing. I'm already excited for your next letter, which I hope will arrive soon.

Wishing you all the best going forward, with lots and lots of love and kisses from

Your Inge, future Gruen

———

Writing to friends such as Inge, Hans, Stefan Pauson, and Muhme, Luzie was, in some way, re-creating her Berlin constellation. She would remain part of their lives, albeit through the somewhat fragile means of letter writing, and they would be part of her life.

There is also the fact that these individuals were not writing to request affidavits, food, funds, or assistance in procuring passage on a ship. How nice it must have been to read Inge's somewhat whimsical and joyous note. In a letter to Inge, Luzie had promised that when the world was open to her again, she was sure to travel and that high on her list of destinations would be the Friedländer family in Bolivia. The statement was probably made with a good deal of humor and hope. Yet when one is dealing with a life full of distress and worry, plans for the future are essential, and kind words from loved ones can lift the spirit, touch the soul, and give one energy to go on.

Cousin Dora

Added to Luzie's responsibilities, which already included her immediate family, cousin Alfons, and aunts Paula and Martha, would be her cousin Dora Hecht. Before introducing Dora, it is worth noting that three of Luzie's four regular correspondents were older women. Aunt Paula Steinberg was approaching sixty, cousin Dora Hecht was sixty-four, and aunt Martha Marchand Harf was fifty. Cousin Alfons Isack was her only steady correspondent who was a male and her contemporary. In terms of both gender and age, the identity of her correspondents was quite skewed. Several factors were at work.

Even before the rise of Nazism, men and women were not of equal numbers in the German Jewish community. There were the many male casualties of World War I, something not unknown to the Hechts, the longer lifespan of women, and the fact that a larger number of men married non-Jews and converted to Christianity. The result was that in 1933 women made up slightly over 52 percent of Germany's Jewish community.[11] Nazism would create conditions that would further skew this ratio.

Overall, fewer women than men escaped Nazi Germany. First of all, a woman simply had a better chance of surviving economically in Germany.[12] As the Nazis drove Jews out of one area of employment after another, one of the few areas that remained open and even expanded a bit due to greater demand was the world of German Jewish social institutions. The Theodor Herzl School, which Luzie's brother, Ralph, attended, for example, went from two hundred students in 1933 to six hundred in 1934.[13] Jewish schools and social service organizations, the pillars of the Jewish communal world, employed teachers, social workers, nurses, clerks, and secretaries—all positions largely thought of as women's professions. A woman might also be able to secure a job in a Jewish home as a housekeeper or nanny. Or as in Luzie's case, there was the possibility of employment in a Jewish-owned enterprise.

"While the employment situation of Jewish women helped keep them in Germany," notes historian Marion Kaplan, "that of men helped them get out."[14] This was something that Luzie experienced firsthand at L. S. Mayer, where executives and salesmen went abroad on business and simply never returned to Germany.

The business world offered more than the opportunity to travel; it enabled the cultivation of contacts outside Germany. Even Luzie, in her five short years at L. S. Mayer as an assistant to an executive, had worked with and communicated with people in Amsterdam, London, and Paris. When the pressure to leave Berlin mounted, she was not shy. She wrote to them all, asking for assistance in leaving Germany. In Luzie's case the answer was never affirmative, but there were some men at the firm, who, through their long years of service and influential positions, had associates abroad who probably proved to be quite precious and helped them emigrate and resettle. Thus, there were instances when it was simply easier for a husband or young adult son to be the first to emigrate. In doing so he was not abandoning his family; there was always the sincere promise that, once settled, he would send for his family.

Another factor working against the "timely flight" of women was the deeply held belief in chivalry, the idea that a man, even a Nazi who would attack Jewish men, would refrain from harming a woman, even if she was Jewish.[15] Indeed, at the beginning stages of Nazi barbarism, the victims were in fact mostly men. On the day after the Kristallnacht pogroms, for example, the thirty thousand Jews arrested by the Nazis were men, not women. Although Jewish women realized that they would be subject to the pain and stress of discrimination and ostracism, they did not imagine that they would be in immediate physical danger.[16]

Ruth Kluger, a Viennese Jew, remembers how her mother "sprang into action" when her father was arrested. "By promising to remain in Austria herself until she could pay the *Reichsfluchtsteuer*, the flight tax, my mother secured his release. My mother made his emigration possible through her promise to stay. But she couldn't find the money to pay the tax, because Jewish real estate had been confiscated and Jewish bank accounts couldn't be accessed by their owners. So we got stuck and he could escape."[17]

Kluger's family experience was not so unusual. A relief worker for the Jewish aid organization HICEM sitting at his Shanghai work desk, typing a report for the home office, commented on a unique feature of the city's Jewish refugee population.[18] "The majority of the refugees from Berlin, Vienna, and Hamburg are men, mostly because they were sent from the concentration camps and were forced to leave Germany. Many have their wives and children here, but many have not."[19] The reason for this, as the HICEM worker alluded, was that the thousands of men incarcerated during Kristallnacht could gain their release from a concentration camp and its daily horrors only if they furnished proof of emigration.

Age also influenced one's ability to flee the Nazis. Even as a healthy young woman who left Berlin at the age of twenty-seven, Luzie was exhausted by the difficulty of the crossing, adjusting to life in a new country, improving her English, and the grinding search for work. There is no puzzle to the fact that younger segments of the Jewish population, better suited to meet the physical and emotional stress of the journey and resettlement, emigrated in larger numbers than the older population. By 1941, two-thirds of the Jews remaining in Germany were past middle age.[20] Dora, Martha, and Paula were part of German Jewry's graying population.

As historian Marion Kaplan notes, the two elements of gender and age worked in concert. "Age, even more than being female, worked against timely flight; together they were lethal."[21] And so there were many reasons why, when Luzie sat down in front of her typewriter to write to a relative back home in Germany, it was likely to be an older female such as her cousin Dora.

Back in Germany, Dora Hecht had probably only been a name, mentioned at a family event every so often. Luzie had never met this older cousin who was in her sixties when Luzie emigrated.

It is not possible to speak of Dora without mentioning her younger sister, Marta, who had married their cousin Leopold Rosenfeld. Perhaps it was this element that had made all three so close, for Leopold was both Dora's brother-in-law and cousin. Marta and Leopold's son, Rudolph, born in 1905, a year after their marriage, was yet another factor tightening their bond. For Dora, who had never married or had children, Rudolph was a prized nephew.

Dora, as well as Marta, Leopold, and Rudolph, lived a considerable distance from Luzie's Berlin home in the Bavarian city of Nuremberg, where in 1923 the Nazis held their first but hardly their most significant rally. A decade later, the city was the site of a massive three-day event, a celebration and statement that the Nazis were now in control. Among those who poured into the city for the 1933 Nuremberg rally were 180,000 Nazi district leaders, 60,000 Hitler Youth, and 10,000 of the black-uniformed SS guards. All future Nazi party congresses, Hitler declared, were to be held in Nuremberg. Life in this city, which pulsated with the Nazi spirit, quickly became intolerable for Luzie's relatives.

In January 1934, Leopold's printing business was Aryanized.

Two months later, Leo, Marta, and Dora moved to the picturesque town of Baden-Baden near the German-French border. A 1928 travel guide describes this as an enchanting town "surrounded by cornfields, vineyards, meadows, woods ... The area offers everything that may rejoice the heart of mankind, and it is indeed one of the most beautiful spots on earth one can imagine."[22]

Perhaps in former days, the area's natural beauty had given Dora spiritual sustenance. But within Germany there was no escape from Nazism. A move to a new town or city might initially afford relief, and Luzie's relatives were hardly the only Jews to try such a tactic, but the respite was bound to be temporary. And so by 1939, the only wish of Dora, her sister Marta, and brother-in-law Leopold was to leave Baden. Their plan was to go to Palestine, where they would join Rudolph, Dora's nephew, who had been living there since 1935. Once again, they would be a united family.

Leopold Rosenfeld's letter to the Baden Foreign Currency Office is testimony to Nazi procedures that ensured that emigrating Jews would exit the country with as little as possible, thereby helping to fill German coffers. Additionally, Rosenfeld's correspondence highlights that those planning to leave were constantly battling the clock, in dread of the thought that arrangements would not be completed before their immigration permits expired.

To: President of Financial Matters (Foreign Currency Office),
Karlsruhe/Baden, Germany
From: Leopold Rosenfeld, Baden-Baden, Germany
Date: January 9, 1939
Translated from the German

September 1939–October 1941

Regarding: Petition for emigrant possessions

I, the signatory, Leopold Israel Rosenfeld was born 8.8. 1873. I am a German citizen, a Jew, and I am married. My wife, Martha Sara Rosenfeld, and my sister-in-law, Dorothea Sara Hecht, are immigrating with me.

Since March 1934, I have resided in Baden-Baden. I am immigrating to Palestine, and I have to leave Germany on February 14, 1939. I have already ordered tickets for a passage from Trieste. Our immigration has to be completed on February 28, 1939.

As of now, I do not know for certain what I will do abroad professionally. I will look for work, and I will accept any position that will allow me to make a living.

I include with this letter:

1. 3 copies of list of my apartment's inventory
2. 3 copies of a list of my baggage
3. 4 copies of a list of my financial assets
4. 3 copies of a list of my jewelry

I am bringing only a few necessary pieces of furnishing with me. I sold my kitchen furniture, which was worth 1200RM, for 300RM. As you can see from my inventory, I purchased a table and a few chairs. I also had to sell my old fridge since the voltage abroad is different; I purchased a new fridge for our new home. The same was true for our stove; there are no gas stoves where we are going. I bought a gasoline stove instead.

The same was true for several electrical gadgets, like the vacuum cleaner and the radio.

I had to sell them in Baden-Baden since the voltage

abroad is different. It was necessary to purchase a lot of new things, and I was forced to exert myself financially.

We used our old sewing machine for almost 50 years. It doesn't work that well, and I would have bought a new sewing machine anyway.

Considering that my immigration permit expires February 28, 1939, I am asking for preferential treatment and speedy permission to export my belongings that are required for me to immigrate.

Leopold Israel Rosenfeld

———

Rudolph had feared that bureaucratic delays would ruin plans for all three to emigrate, but the problem that did arise came from an entirely different direction. His sister-in-law Dora's heart illness flared, forcing her to cancel her passage to Palestine. By now ship tickets were precious; with thousands clamoring to get out of Germany, demand far exceeded the number of spaces.

Her heart ailment cruelly robbed Dora of the chance to emigrate with her family. She stayed behind and watched as her sister and brother-in-law packed their bags and left Nazi Germany without her. Perhaps she would join them in the future, but in the meantime she was left alone in Baden-Baden and in need of assistance. Dora was one more Hecht, in a growing list of relatives, who turned to Arnold Hatch in Albany.

Because Arnold knew only English and Dora only German, he gave Luzie the dual task of translating Dora's letters and writing his responses. So now, when they were no longer even on the same continent, Dora and Luzie, cousins who had never met, were to become acquainted.

September 1939–October 1941

—

Dora Hecht sent Arnold her first letter in August 1939, nine months after Kristallnacht, describing a life of nerve-racking uncertainty, fear of never being reunited with her loved ones, dreary hours, and a loneliness that was hard to bear.

Given that Luzie had never had any contact with Dora, when she first wrote, she needed to introduce herself, explaining her place in the sprawling Hecht family tree.

———

To: Dora Hecht, Baden-Baden, Germany
From: Luzie Hatch, New York
Date: September 21, 1939
Translated from the German

Dear Miss Hecht:

On behalf of Arnold Hatch, I am writing to confirm receipt of your letter to him dated August 8th.

I was in Albany at Aunt Alice's funeral (I am the daughter of Edwin Hecht, son of Felix Hecht) . . . There [at the funeral] Arnold asked me to respond to you since of course he cannot write in German. He was very happy to read your letter . . .

However, in reading your letter, he did not find the answer to the questions he had asked you . . . Please let him know promptly, very precisely and in detail, what assets you have at your disposal, what you need to live, i.e., including apartment, food, clothing, doctors, etc., and to what extent you are supported by your relatives. I hope you understand what Arnold wants to know and that you will give him the information as soon as possible.

I hope that you are receiving satisfactory reports from your relatives. Unfortunately, my parents' writings from Shanghai are not very encouraging.

I would like to take this opportunity to extend to you my best wishes for the New Year,

Your Luzie

———

Through their letter writing, Dora and Luzie would begin to build a relationship. Dora's request at the end of her response, that Luzie use the pronoun reserved for close friends and family, indicates this growing bond.

———

To: Luzie Hatch, New York
From: Dora Hecht, Baden-Baden, Germany
Date: November 8, 1939
Translated from the German

Dear Lucie,

For the letter that I received from you yesterday, I would like to promptly express my deepest gratitude. The interest that you express makes me very happy, and that you are interested in my well-being: I will gladly answer your questions.

Health wise, my heart is not improving. When one doesn't have one's own home, illness is twice as severe.

My passage by ship was canceled since I was unable to travel. The balance was refunded to me yesterday . . . Today I also received a disbursement of 400 marks for monthly expenses paid in full. With that I can meet my expenses and cover the medicine that I require as a result of my ailment.

As you know, I have been accustomed to living economically since my youth. Dear Arnold's sympathy is moving; it is comforting to have a benefactor in one's hour of need.

Thanking you again for your kind letter. I ask you to send my regards to all of our loved ones. I am sorry that Ida cannot write to me. In your next letter I hope to be addressed with "you."

With all my love and good-bye,

Your Dora

———

By the winter of 1940, Dora was contending not simply with a heart ailment and a miserable sense of loneliness but with the most basic need of all, the need for food.

Her situation was not unusual. As early as the spring of 1939 there were reports of sudden food shortages throughout western Germany, Dora's home. In preparation for war, the government had been buying and storing food, diminishing the quantities of food that made it to the marketplace. When war came, it inevitably brought with it food rationing, which was, of course, far more severe for the Jewish population.

Jews were assigned limited shopping hours, a restriction almost impossible to avoid because Dora's ration card, like that of all Jews, had been stamped with a "J." In those days, before supermarkets, shoppers went from store to store, the butcher to the baker. But with long queues and short hours to shop, how much could be accomplished? And then there was the fact that Jews were required to shop toward the end of the day and thus at times reached the front of the line only to discover that the food was sold out.

Hoping to augment her food supply, Dora had written to her sister, Marta Rosenfeld, in Palestine and requested "Libby's," a popular canned food brand. The letter set off a chain reaction of alarm. Marta wrote to Eda, Arnold's paternal aunt in New York City, who spoke German, asking her to have Arnold ship some food off to Germany. Eda, in turn, sent the letter to Luzie requesting that she contact Arnold. In the end, Dora's request for food originally sent to Palestine was forwarded to Eda in Manhattan, than to Luzie in Queens, New York, and finally onto Arnold in Albany. It was a long, circuitous route for a piece of pressing information.

––––

To: Arnold Hatch, Albany, New York
From: Luzie Hatch, New York
Date: January 7, 1940

Dear Arnold:

I hope you are well . . . Aunt Eda got a letter from her niece Marta from Palestine and wanted me to inform you of it. Here is the part that Aunt Eda wanted translated and forwarded to you.

> You can imagine how glad I was to hear after 10 weeks directly from Dora . . . I understand the contents of her letter very well and am in a position to explain the error about the "Libby's." With this she meant food in cans which Arnold may send her. This request worries me very much because I learn from it what she is lacking. It is terrible that we are

not able to help her in this direction, but I hope that my dear cousins Arnold and Stephen might be in a position to comply with her wish.

Of course, I do not want to make any suggestions, but it seems rather doubtful to me whether Dora ever would receive any food sent to her from this country. As far as I have learned, the addressee has to acknowledge receipt of such parcels in order to bluff the sender, and then is compelled by the Gestapo (Secret Police) to hand over all or the biggest part to the "Winterhilfswerk" [German winter relief fund, which excluded Jews]. I thought it my duty to give you this information, of course, without any intention of influencing your decision.

Yours, as ever,

Luzie

———

It is not known whether Arnold sent Dora some "Libby's" or perhaps, given his practical nature, settled instead on wiring funds. In any event, by spring, Dora would write with a new request: she wanted to come to America.

———

To: Arnold Hatch, Albany, New York
From: Luzie Hatch, New York
Date: April 9, 1940

Dear Arnold:
I am attaching translation of Dora Hecht's letter [request to come to America].

Yesterday, I received news from Shanghai which gave me a very bad time. It seems my parents have been without means for some weeks . . . As you know my father does not feel well and instead of getting rest which he needs so badly, he peddled with soap and cravats in order to earn a few cents. As, in the meantime, they will have received the money you sent them middle of February, I hope that everything is better.

The situation in Europe is terrible. Everybody is crying for help. Did you decide anything about Alfons Isack's case? I heard that he does not know how to arrange to leave Germany, and I am trying to find a way for him, but until now without success.

I hope that it will be possible to send Aunt Martha the missing papers soon so that she and her sweet little daughter can be saved. Isn't there any way to get the tax return from Washington very soon now?

Aunt Martha asked in one of her letters whether she should bring furniture, chinaware, linen, etc. along. As far as I am informed the transportation costs for this have to be paid from here. Therefore, we would appreciate to have your opinion . . .

To close this letter with one pleasant thing . . . I got a raise of $2.50. This is not much, but nevertheless it was a great joy for me because it proved the interest taken in me.

I am looking forward to seeing you soon and am with best regards, also for your family,

Your cousin Luzie

———

September 1939–October 1941

—

164

To: Luzie Hatch, New York
From: Arnold Hatch, Albany, New York
Date: April 11, 1940

Dear Luzie:

This will acknowledge receipt of your letter dated April 9th to which was attached a translation of the letter from Dora. Now, it is not practical to even attempt to bring her [Dora] over here at the present time. In the first place, and of paramount importance, is the fact that according to her letter she has just applied last October to the U.S. Consulate for a registration number. This means that she must be very far down on the list and actually has not a chance of getting a visa within a reasonable time.

On top of all that, her age and physical condition are against her and make it inadvisable, to say the least, to even try to bring her over here. Actually, I haven't the heart to write her all this, but I wish that you would write her a letter, telling her anything that you like—perhaps that I am not feeling very well and have asked you to write in my place. Tell her that if the 400 marks a month which she is allotted is ever discontinued that she is to let me know and we will endeavor to make some arrangements to send her some money if wartime conditions permit.

You must also break the news to her that it is not feasible at the present time to send her an affidavit because, between us, it would not do the slightest good, and there is no sense in going through all that trouble for something which will not work out.

Again, referring to your own letter, there is nothing

that I can do at present time about Alfons Isack. I doubt very much if a young man like that will ever get out of Germany under present wartime conditions. It is unfortunate but there is nothing I can do for him at present.

Now, as regards your parents I am very sorry indeed ... that they and Rolf have been having such a terrible time, but I do wish that when you write me you would be just a little more definite about some things that I have been anxious to know.

You say that only a day or two ago you had a letter from them, but you do not make it clear whether they have received the money which I sent them in the middle of February or whether they have not received it ... Now if you know that they got it, please say so in plain English. I can not tell from your letter whether you know that they received it or whether you think they should have received it by this time.

I am also interested in learning ... what progress is being made about their visas ... and getting them out of Shanghai. You say nothing about that either. I repeat that if anything gets cleared up so that they can get out of there we shall take care of the financial arrangements just as soon as things are set.

Now, relative to the additional papers required by the American Consulate at Stuttgart concerning Martha Marchand Harf and her daughter, I just received today the certified copy of my 1938 Federal Tax Return. I, therefore, send you enclosed the papers requested in Mrs. Freidman's letter to me ... and I ask that you turn these papers over to her and assist her in sending them to the American Council at Stuttgart. The papers being sent are:

1. Certified copy of the latest Federal Income Tax Return

2. Statement covering all the other matters demanded by the Consulate.

I trust that these papers will supply everything needed, and you can arrange to have them forwarded to Germany at once.

I am very much pleased to note about your raise, and I congratulate you. You have done very well in a little over a year since you are in this country, and I am proud of you.

With much love, and hoping that everything in this letter is now clear, I am

Yours, as ever,

Arnold

P.S. As regards Martha and her daughter bringing over their furniture, chinaware, linens, etc., when they are finally released, the answer to that is a great big 'No.' They might better sacrifice this stuff than pay all the transportation costs on a lot of stuff which is probably worth mighty little to transport across the ocean.

———

———

To: Dora Hecht, Baden-Baden, Germany
From: Luzie Hatch, New York
Date: May 2, 1940
Translated from the German

Dear Dora,

Since, as you know, he cannot write in German, Arnold has asked me this time again to confirm receipt of your last letter to him—which of course I am quite happy to do. We speak of you often here, and I would certainly write more if I wasn't so very overloaded with work and with a terribly extensive correspondence.

Arnold was happy to receive your letter. He would like you to know that you should immediately notify him should the monthly allocation of 400 Reichsmarks ever not come through for any reason. He will then try to make other arrangements if it is in any way possible. I believe this will surely be a great reassurance to you.

Regarding your request filing an affidavit, Arnold is of the opinion that since you did not receive your registration number until October 1939, you cannot count on receiving a summons to the consulate for another few years. For that reason he would like to defer this whole question until it becomes really acute. At the same time, he would like to point out to you that he has now filed so many affidavits that lately difficulties have set in, and for that reason he does not know yet if he is in the position to file any more.

The last time that I wrote to you, I was out of work. However, shortly thereafter, I promptly found work again, and I am happy that I earn enough to feed myself without any assistance.

Unfortunately, I have only bad news from my parents in Shanghai. I only hope that they will be able to come here soon, so that I can fatten up my father for a start. I'm sure your relatives are writing to you diligently—hopefully they are somewhat content.

September 1939–October 1941

—

So dear Dora, take good care of yourself and with all my love.

Your

Luzie

———

A Persistent Cousin

Cousin Alfons was determined to leave Germany and he wrote repeatedly for assistance. An element contributing to this persistence must have been the knock on his door from a Nazi official investigating a supposed "deceptive declaration of assets." Alfons had allegedly failed to list 2,500 in reichsmarks, a violation of the ordinance of April 26, 1938, requiring a complete registration of Jewish assets.

His perceived lack of cooperation irritated the interrogator, a point the Nazi official made clear in a report to the Gestapo. "During the entirety of the police interrogation, Isack exhibited an arrogant and impudent behavior. He was adamant in his denial, and only after a long interrogation did he eventually deign to tell the truth. Apparently he will stop at nothing in his efforts to mislead the authorities."[23]

Alfons claimed that he no longer had the 2,500 reichsmarks, stating that the bulk of the sum, 2,000 marks, had been stolen and the remainder spent.[24] Fortunately, the proceedings were suspended.[25] At least for the moment, Alfons was spared imprisonment.

In Alfons's correspondence there is no mention of either his first arrest during Kristallnacht or his interrogation in the winter of 1940. Most certainly these were willful omissions. It was no secret that censors opened mail, searching for those disloyal to the state so that they could feel the hand of Nazi justice and be removed from society. In her memoir, Frieda Sichel aptly described how fear had enveloped and pressed in on the German Jewish community. "Every evening I thought about the day that has just passed and asked myself if I had done or said anything that could endanger my husband or myself."[26] The significant caution that ruled spoken words was even greater for written words, which, once committed to paper, could not be denied.

Perhaps if Arnold had known of Alfons's expanding Gestapo file he would have been more amenable to his requests. That is a question that remains open. But there can be no doubt that these repeated encounters with Nazi authorities increased Alfons's determination to escape Germany.

He had gone to the Hilfsverein, where he listed both Luzie and Arnold as his relations in the United States. The Hilfsverein in turn contacted the Hebrew Immigrant Aid Society (HIAS) in New York, instructing them to contact Alfons's American relatives. Thus, in the spring of 1940, both Luzie and Arnold received letters from the HIAS, which although short on specifics claimed that emigration might be possible if they agreed to cover Alfons's travel expenses. "Brief, vague, and inconclusive" was how Arnold described the letter. Despite the organization's solid reputation, which he freely acknowledged, Arnold would do nothing on the basis of this "meager information." Still, he did not simply toss the matter aside but wrote to the HIAS asking for clarification.

September 1939–October 1941

—

To: Hebrew Sheltering and Immigrant Aid Society, New York

From: Arnold Hatch, Albany, New York

Date: April 19, 1940

Gentlemen:

This will acknowledge receipt of your letter dated April 16th with reference to Alfons Israel Isack, Essen Kopstadtplatz 1. I have a large number of guarantees, affidavits, and financial advance on my hands at the present time, but regardless of that will be willing to go into this a little further, if you will supply something more than the very vague information contained in your letter just received. I should like to know definitely the following things:

1. For the sum of $400.00, is your organization definitely certain that the party in question can be gotten out of Essen into a neutral country?

2. Into what neutral country is it planned to send him?

3. Has he a high emigration quota number, so that he would be released quickly, and if so, how quickly?

4. Would anything else to accomplish the desired result be required aside from the sum of $400.00?

Since you have initiated this matter, I should like some really definite detailed information covering all of the above matters and anything else that you see fit to supply before going into this further.

Yours very truly,

Arnold Hatch

To: Arnold Hatch, Albany, New York
From: Hebrew Sheltering and Immigrant Aid Society, New York
Date: May 7, 1940

Re: Alfons Israel Isack
Essen Kopstadtplatz 1

Dear Mr. Hatch:

In reply to your letter of April 19th, please be advised that the above named can emigrate to Shanghai if you will make available the sum of $400.00.

We have no information concerning his quota number. We assume that it must be a high one, or else he would wait in Germany until his turn is reached in the quota.

Therefore, will you kindly advise us whether you will make this sum available to him.

Very sincerely yours,
for Isaac L. Asofsky,
Executive Director

To: Arnold Hatch, Albany, New York
From: Luzie Hatch, New York
Date: May 6, 1940

Dear Arnold:

Only at the end of last week I had a chance to see Mr. Asofsky of the HIAS with reference to Alfons Isack's emigration. I was informed that the HIAS only acts as mediator for the Hilfsverein in Germany, and that it is their task to communicate with people here according to the advice of the Hilfsverein. Therefore, the HIAS does not know in every case to which country people are going to be sent, but inquires, of course, about the intentions if this is requested.

I was told furthermore that in case the Hilfsverein or the HIAS do not succeed in bringing Alfons Isack out of Germany the requested deposit would be refunded. I asked that this information be given to you in writing. All particulars about this case have to be given from the Hilfsverein in Germany, and the HIAS will submit them to you as soon as they will have been received. I was told that your letter to them of April 19 would get an adequate answer . . . I am sorry that I could not accomplish much, but, of course, I am willing to do everything I can in order to facilitate matters.

I availed myself of the good opportunity and again discussed the case of my parents. Mr. Asofsky [HIAS worker] is of the opinion that their turn for getting a visa should be right now as everywhere the American Consuls are now calling those people who have registered in August 1938.

I also spoke to him about their fare . . . So he told me that if, for instance, three quarters of the required amount would be deposited with them they would get in touch with the Committee in Shanghai to ask that they provide the balance. He cannot predict the result because the Committee . . . has been having very great financial troubles. But still, I think a trial should be worthwhile if the time comes. What is your opinion?

Yours, as ever,

Luzie

———

The Fateful Hour

When Germany invaded Poland on September 1, 1939, the British and French responded two days later with a declaration of war. Yet months would pass without any major combat, causing some at the time to label it the Phony War. All that would change on May 10, 1940, when with lightning speed German troops invaded Belgium, the Netherlands, and Luxembourg while the Luftwaffe bombed targets in France. German victory would be brutal and swift. In Luxembourg there had been no significant resistance, and by noon of the invasion day the Nazis would occupy the capital. By the end of May, the Netherlands and Belgium had both capitulated. The French would surrender on June 22. Writing of the May Blitzkreig, the *New York Times* stated that "the static conflict of the West" had become a total war.

Repeatedly, Arnold had stated that he would bring his relatives to America when the "air had cleared." But the hostilities, rather than subsiding, had escalated, finally exploding into a war that would drag on for years. The spread of war would make their lives in Germany more dangerous and their chance of escape more complicated as overland and shipping routes, once accessible, would close.

To: Luzie Hatch, New York
From: Arnold Hatch, Albany, New York
Date: May 20, 1940

Dear Luzie:

I enclose herewith an Air Mail letter just received from Alfons Isack.

Dear Arnold,

Once more I have to apply to you with a request to

help me to emigrate. I often wrote to you but without getting any answer from you. Did you not receive my letters? I have nobody else abroad who can assist me for leaving this country. I only confide in your support.

For I have no registered for U.S., I intend to go to South America because a brother of my aunt, living in Chile, has demanded me; but he is not in the position to pay the passage, therefore I ask you to place the necessary money to my disposal for the voyage.

Of course as soon as possible I will pay back the money, then I am not afraid of any work. I am new working as a navvy.

I am sure you read the leading article in our Jewish newspaper. Please, open the door for my emigration by your help. That is my urgent request. I hope you and your folks are very well and I send you all my heartiest regards. Please let me have your answer immediately.

Your affectionate
Cousin Alfons

I wish that you would write him and tell him that under present conditions I am unable to do anything for him. The whole business is much too indefinite for me, and on top of that I have saddled myself with so many obligations that I cannot assume anymore. Besides, I do not think that in spite of any efforts that we might make that we would get him out of Germany under present conditions.

Perhaps, at some future time and in a happier day, when the air has cleared a little bit and I have less on my shoulders, I may be able to do something for him but not at present. I will appreciate it very much if you will write him this to him tactfully.

With much love to you, Herta, and Aunt Eda, I am,

Yours, as ever, Arnold

——

Following Arnold's instructions, Luzie wrote to her cousin Alfons not only relaying Arnold's thoughts but apologizing for the delay in her response. Luzie had left her residence in Washington Heights, Manhattan, and settled into a studio apartment in Queens, and her search for the new apartment had taken some time.

——

To: Alfons Isack, Essen, Germany
From: Luzie Hatch, New York
Date: August 2, 1940
Translated from the German

My Dear Alfons:

As you will see from the above address, I have moved. The move and other professional and personal events have entailed much work and much agitation, so that it is only today that I have a chance to write you in detail.

No you mustn't think that I haven't thought about you all the time in the meantime, and that I haven't made any efforts on your behalf. To the contrary, it is in part because I wanted to give you a favorable, definitive answer that I haven't written you sooner.

I have been in touch with Arnold Hatch and with the organization in consideration; Hebrew Sheltering and Immigrant Aid Society (HIAS), several times on your behalf.

——

I have visited the organization in order to find out everything for you, and unfortunately I have to give you the following answer:

1) Answer from Arnold: Arnold received your letter of May 8th of this year, and since he cannot write in German, he has asked me to write to you on his behalf. Unfortunately at present, Arnold sees no way of helping you, all the more so since in his opinion, there is no way to travel overseas at the moment.

He knows that it is your greatest wish to be reunited with your relatives in South America, and wants to let you know emphatically that he is in no way averse to helping you at a later point, once everything has been resolved somewhat and one can see things more clearly.

To this I have to say that of course I am more than sorry that I cannot give you a more positive answer. But on the other hand, I am still very hopeful that at a somewhat later date, Arnold will take on your situation. As you know, it took me a long time before I achieved anything as well.

In any case you can count on me to continue to make efforts on your behalf, and as soon as I see even a small opportunity of some sort, I will immediately get in touch with Arnold and with you.

As for you, I recommend that you contact Arnold again from time to time. But before you do that, I would get in touch with the aid association, so that you can give Arnold very precise specifications: what you need, where you want to go, i.e. where you can go, when you could leave, etc.

2) Answer from HIAS: they told me that at the moment immigration to South America is not at all as easy as

you described it in your letter. Please immediately have the aid association give you the exact information: what is needed, where you can go, and what modes of transportation are available.

The aid association got in touch with the organization here on your behalf, not for South America, but rather for Shanghai. Now, unfortunately I know only too well how dreadful it is in Shanghai, and therefore I do not want you to end up there; that also entails high costs, and then you would surely have no future there.

So again: my advice is: get back in touch with the aid association immediately, have them tell you exactly what opportunities there are to get to South America, how much money is required for travel and for the entry permit, etc. Then get back in touch with me and with Arnold again.

Write to Arnold and tell him that I told you that at the moment he does not see any way of helping you, but that you hope, nevertheless, that he will be able to do something for you at a later date that you promise to make good on it, etc.

I know that those letters are not pleasant to write. But yet you must keep trying, and as I said, I will not forget you and will look out for any opportunity.

Please send all my love to Aunt Julchen, Uncle Siegmund, Aunt Lina, Uncle Max.

I also thank you very much for your kind letter of May 2nd that arrived punctually on my birthday. It was awfully nice of you to think of my birthday. I am also very ashamed that I didn't congratulate you. Nevertheless, I mean very, very well with you and hope to be able to prove it as well.

September 1939–October 1941

—

Please write back immediately. I will answer promptly as well. Unfortunately I have to end today, not because I don't want to write more [rest of letter is cut off.]

———

After she wrote to Alfons Isack, next in line was Aunt Paula Steinberg. As Luzie admitted, her letter was long overdue.

———

To: Paula Steinberg, Dortmund, Germany
From: Luzie Hatch, New York
Date: August 8, 1940
Translated from the German

My dear Aunt Paula,

This letter has already been written countless times in my mind. I didn't want to fob you off with a short card . . . I have resolved to at least occasionally send you greetings via postcard, so that you will see that you are still my favorite aunt, and that you are <u>especially close to my heart</u>.

Congratulations on your newly achieved honor of being a grandma, and I wish with all my heart that you will soon find much happiness with your children and grandchildren. Has Walter opened his own pub in the meantime, or is he still helping Erna and Gustav?

Healthwise, I hope you are well. Hold on to the courage that you have shown throughout your life—it will and must work out. I don't know what your current prospects are for joining your children.

It did hurt my feelings somewhat that you could even assume that I might have considered your request for assistance to be inappropriate. You must know me well enough to know that I am very concerned about you. However, it is unlikely that I will be able to get my cousin to help with it, since it was already difficult enough to secure my parents' voyage.

But first of all, there is an organization here that might contribute a portion: and second, one must see what Aunt Emma, I, and maybe other friends and relatives that you have here (and that you will please list for me) can pool together when the time comes. Where there is a will, there is a way.

I also read your letter to Aunt Emma. If I understand correctly, you have a number on the waiting list for the United States. Is that true? How high is it? Do you have a chance of receiving an affidavit? Please answer all these questions for me, and if you would even consider the possibility of immigrating here.

Even if I don't write so often, my thoughts are <u>with you a lot</u>, and you will always be able to count on me. I would be very hurt if you did not turn to me. You know, my whole life, I have always seen you almost as a second mother.

And even if I didn't love you as much as I do, the memory of my dear mother would not permit me to ever forsake you. If ever fate should have it that your path leads you here, you will always find a home with me. I would consider myself lucky to have you around me.

Are you living comfortably? How is the food? Do you cook for yourself? Please write to me about this as well.

I will have my picture taken shortly and will mail you a little photograph so that you know how I look now. By the way, I don't have a single picture of you, and I ask you <u>please</u> to enclose one at the next opportunity. But please do it!!

When you come here, you must bring along some turnip top seeds. Then we will introduce this dish here and certainly be very successful with it.

With heartfelt greetings and kisses from your loving

Luzie

Even as she dealt with the needs and fears of those left in Germany, Alfons Isack, Dora Hecht, Paula Steinberg, and Martha Marchand Harf, Luzie needed to assist her immediate family in Shanghai. They were, understandably, her primary responsibility.

10

The Shanghai Solution

In early August, Luzie visited two shipping companies, hoping to secure passage from Shanghai to the United States for her family. At each office she dutifully took out a notepad and recorded the information. "Booked for six months including first class. Do not accept any application for the next 5 months" was what she heard at the Nippon Line. She underlined the disappointing information with thick and long pencil strokes. The story at the American President Lines was the same, no openings, even for first class, and no future applications being accepted.

It was disheartening news for a young woman who not only

missed her family, after being separated for nearly two years, but worried about their very survival. Clearly, she wanted them out of Shanghai, where her brother had come close to death after contracting paratyphoid fever, her father's health was poor, and the family's financial situation was bleak.

So when a work colleague told her about a Mr. Hammerschlag at the North American Travel League who, for a substantial fee, could do what seemed impossible—get passage for her family almost immediately—she jumped at the chance and informed Arnold at once. He responded promptly to her proposal.

To: Luzie Hatch, The Westholm, Stamford, CT
From: Arnold Hatch, Albany, New York
Date: August 13, 1940

Dear Luzie:

I have your letter of August 12, and I know that you are worried and pretty despondent over the whole thing. However, the plan as submitted is so utterly ridiculous and even worse that I would not consider it for a minute. The chances are that the celebrated Mr. Hammerschlag is nothing more or less than what we call here a 'ticket speculator.' Nothing can be found out about him of the North American Travel League, Inc., and in addition it may or may not have occurred to you that these are very, very bad times indeed for Americans to be entering into mysterious deals with Germans.

I do not mean to be abrupt, but in returning the enclosed papers I am forced to tell you that not for one minute would I consider any such absurd arrangement as is mentioned in these letters.

In brief then, as much as I hate to admit it to myself, there is nothing to be done. However, visas can be extended, and I would suggest that you write your father by Air Mail telling him to extend his visas from time to time until this utterly impossible situation rectified itself if it ever does.

I realize that all this is terribly discouraging, but I will not go ahead with any such thing as the North American Travel League because it is risky and dangerous—not only from the money angle, but from other angles as well. There is no need to make yourself ill over this thing because it is just one of those circumstances that cannot be helped.

With much love to you, Aunt Eda, and Herta, I am

Yours, as ever,

Arnold

———

Shortly after Arnold torpedoed the North American Travel League proposition, another possibility came up. This time Luzie would not let the opportunity slip away. She did not stop to ask Arnold for permission or guidance but simply pushed forward on her own. While the first plan had involved an unfamiliar character, Mr. Hammerschlag of the North American Travel League, Luzie was now dealing with a Mr. Plaut, an agent she knew well and trusted.

She wasted no time. Using all her charm, Luzie borrowed money from a neighbor and coworkers, took the fifty dollars she had managed to save, and purchased the tickets. Only after it had all been completed did she inform Arnold. As always, she made sure to offer the proper deference.

———

To: Arnold Hatch, Albany, New York
From: Luzie Hatch, New York
Date: August 23, 1940

Dear Arnold:

I am very sorry that I did not express myself clearly when I spoke to you over the telephone last Tuesday. I intended to give you a detailed report about the whole transaction after its completion and understood that this met with your approval.

The situation is as follows:

I got in touch with Mr. Plaut of Plaut Travel, whom I know personally. He told me that if I were in a position to decide quickly, he might be able to obtain passage for my family. He got in touch with the American President Lines, and when I called him on Tuesday he informed me that he was able to arrange for accommodations for my parents and brother, but I had to decide the same day.

As you know I tried very much to get you, but could reach you only at about 7 o'clock in the evening. The next morning I called Mr. Plaut in order to book those accommodations, but they were gone. He again communicated with the American President Lines. The same day I was told that he had succeeded in getting other accommodations, and this time, I accepted at once.

It is the rule that the passage has to be paid at once. So

on August 21st, I gave to Mr. Plaut a check for $100.00 which I borrowed from Mr. Colman, and another $50.00 in cash of my own money. Yesterday I called and promised to pay the balance for today.

This morning Mr. Friedmann loaned me another $115.00 and then our office manager gave me $150.00. The remainder I got from one of the men at the office who very generously offered to help with a check for $354.00, so that I was able to settle the whole passage. Of course, before I paid Mr. Plaut, friends of mine checked on his reliability in Dun and Bradstreet's.

My parents have to sleep in third class accommodations but are entitled to Tourist Class food and other privileges. The fare is $220.00 from Kobe to San Francisco plus $20.00 from Shanghai to Kobe. The rail fare from San Francisco to New York is $53.83.

Today I sent a cable to my parents informing them that they are to sail with *S/S President Coolidge* and to get in touch with the American President Lines over there. I was informed that people are not permitted to take money out of China. So I think I shall cable them only a small amount, maybe $50.00 to cover their current expenses, and perhaps the transportation of their few belongings.

It may be necessary to remit to them some money as soon as they land in San Francisco, but this, of course, does not have to be taken care of at this moment.

I hope, dear Arnold, that this settles everything and that you are satisfied with the report. Of course, I am willing to give you any further information you may want.

September 1939–October 1941
—

Otherwise everything is fine. Now I am enjoying my work again, everybody is nice to me.

I am, with much love and best regards to you and your family,

Yours, as ever,

Luzie

———

———

To: Luzie Hatch, New York

From: Arnold Hatch, Albany, New York

Date: August 24, 1940

Dear Luzie:

I have your letter of August 23rd, and while obviously I do not know anything at all about the people with whom you have made these arrangements, nevertheless I have enough confidence in you to feel reasonably sure that you would not let yourself in for anything which involved a lot of money and was not perfectly secure. Your experience working where you are, and the investigations that you made, appear perfectly satisfactory to you, and therefore I am satisfied also, relying on your judgment.

In the meanwhile, I am sorry that you had all this trouble and running around, which in a way is really your own fault because I was waiting to receive from you earlier the information which I just got today. However, there is probably no harm done. You can repay the loans that you got from these various people out of the check enclosed herewith, and you are not to worry about the thing unnecessarily. If everything goes as we all hope, your parents will get out of that hellhole and be in New York before very long.

I am sure that you are very much relieved and happy over the fortunate break which enabled you to get accommodations for your family.

With much love, I am

Yours, in haste,

Arnold

———

———

To: Arnold Hatch, Albany, New York
From: Luzie Hatch, New York
Date: August 26, 1940

Dear Arnold:

I thank you very, very much for your letter of August 24th with the generous check. You can imagine how thankful I am to you and Stephen for making it possible for my family to come to this country where they can live in peace—I am sure that they never will forget what you did for them. I appreciate your confidence in me and you may be assured that I am handling the whole matter with utmost care.

The *S. S. President Coolidge* is leaving Shanghai on September 10th, and supposed to arrive in San Francisco about September 26th. I shall inform you of the exact date of the arrival. The railroad tickets will be sent on board of the ship when landing in San Francisco.

I shall keep you informed about everything.

September 1939–October 1941
—

I hope that you are feeling well and are not working too hard.

With much love and best regards, I am,

Yours, as ever,

Luzie

———

11

Rosh Hashana,
1940

September, the month of the Jewish New Year, brought Luzie what she hoped for most, the arrival of her family in the United States. They had finally made it to America, albeit their route had included a challenging eighteen months in Shanghai. Once their ship docked in San Francisco, the family faced the last leg of their journey, a cross-country train trip that likely took seven days. Their reunion was a heartwarming event. Other developments, however, brought distress rather than joy.

Cousin Dora feared that she would be losing her financial support, the allowance from her brother-in-law Leopold's estate. When his business had been Aryanized in Nuremberg, Leopold had been fortunate enough to receive a decent price. But when he and his wife, Dora's sister, left for Palestine, they were allowed to take only ten reichsmarks along with some money for the ship. The proceeds from his business sale stayed behind in Germany in a blocked account. In some way, perhaps because she was a close relative and had Leopold's consent, Dora had been able to withdraw small sums from his bank account in Baden. These funds allowed her to scrape by. But in this letter she relayed her alarm that she was no longer able to access his account.

To: Arnold Hatch, Albany, New York
From: Dora Hecht, Baden-Baden, Germany
Date: August 24, 1940
Translated from the German

Dear Arnold!

Aunt Ida wrote me about your concern for my health. Of course, I am also aware of that from your kind letters. That is delightful and comforting to me.

One big concern has been weighing on me for the past few days. I heard that the financial support that was accorded to me from Uncle Leo's estate until now has been terminated. I don't know if this provision is permanent or only temporary. Leo lives in Palestine; that is a hostile country. [Palestine was under the mandate of Great Britain, a nation at war with Germany.]

For the longest time I haven't heard anything from my loved ones. I can only continue to wish and hope that they are well.

As you can imagine, I am now living in a state of great

Rosh Hashana, 1940
—

apprehension when I think about the future, and I am addressing myself to you with the question whether it would be possible for you to assist me in this time of need. Would you be able to send me 400 marks per month, and in fact, could you send me the first installment by telephone?

It is not easy for me to express this request, but for the time being I see no other recourse. I will keep you posted with regard to my well-being going forward. But the thought that I am not totally abandoned gives me renewed strength time and time again.

I send my love to you and your whole family, also Aunt Ida and Herta, as well as Lucie from all my heart.

Your lonely Dora

—

Meanwhile, Cousin Martha Harf had written Arnold of her new plan for leaving Germany. She and her daughter, Ruthi, would travel by train from Germany to Moscow, where they would then take the Trans-Siberian Railroad to the Russian port of Vladivostok. If there were no problems, the train trek across Russia and Siberia would take twelve to thirteen days. At Vladivostok they would book passage on a ship to Shanghai and from there would eventually travel on to the United States.

—

To: Luzie Hatch, New York
From: Arnold Hatch, Albany, New York
Date: August 28, 1940

Dear Luzie:

The other day I received a cable from Martha Harf,

which when translated said that I should pay immediately certain undefined sums to the American Express Company. The whole thing was so jumbled, incoherent, and impractical that I sent it down to the American Express Company in New York and asked them to advise me what all this meant, etc.

I have just received their reply which I send you herewith. Now, it is utterly impractical at this time to send two women from Cologne via Berlin, Moscow, Siberia, and Japan or even by the other overland routing to Lisbon. The steamers are packed. The journey is hazardous and uncertain, and the American Express Company in accepting the utterly impossible sum of $700.00 per person does not guarantee a thing except that they will return your money in case transportation cannot be arranged.

It appears to me that Martha, more or less naturally, is so anxious to get herself and her daughter out of Germany that she is getting hysterical about it, for which in a way you cannot blame her. However, I cannot and will not go ahead with any such vague plan as this, and I want either you or Mrs. Friedmann to write her at once, by air mail if necessary, that the plan must be dropped for the time being.

Please have someone write her not to waste her money on cables because this whole nebulous plan is out so far as I am concerned, and I will not sanction it, and that is final. You can probably see for yourself that the cost of this thing outside of the uncertainty of it is perfectly ridiculous.

All of the foregoing means that things will just have to wait until this war is over, if it ever is, and I would really

Rosh Hashana, 1940

—

much prefer not to be bothered by these wild plans in the meanwhile. Things in the world are so uncertain that I cannot get into plans as insane as the above mentioned. Just as an example of how uncertain things are, we sent through a reputable bank some money to the Rosenfelds [Dora's family] in Palestine, which is not in the immediate war zone, back in May, and so far the bank has not been able to show delivery of this money.

I appreciate that when either you or Mrs. Friedmann [Martha's daughter] write to Martha she will be bitterly disappointed, but there is nothing else that can be done for the time being. I did not start this war, and I cannot finish it, and I cannot change the conditions that result from it.

With much love to you, I am

Arnold

―――

Although Luzie abided by Arnold's instructions, she bent them slightly, suggesting to Martha a way of appealing to his personality.

―――

To: Martha Harf, Cologne, Germany

From: Luzie Hatch, New York

Date: August 30, 1940

Translated from the German

My dear Aunt Martha:

This letter encloses a very disappointing message for you unfortunately, and I am dreadfully sorry that I must write this note.

Arnold showed me a copy of his letter to you … Well, you should have already received this letter and know that Arnold is against you going on the long, burdensome and expensive trip over Russia and Japan.

I want to give you a personal advice now. I have information for you. I have found out that the journey through Russia has so far often been sponsored by the "Hilfsverein" [German Jewish Aid Society]. Please contact the "Hilfsverein" immediately to work this out for you.

I strongly believe it might be easier to have Arnold do something if one could tell him that funding until Japan is ensured. I am sorry, this is the only advice I am able to give you at the moment. I know that even with the trip to Japan secured, from a financial perspective, Arnold still will not like the idea of you undertaking the long journey over Russia. But according to my feeling and opinion, it would be much easier to change his mind in that case and just make him finance the trip from Japan to here.

I want to point out, however, that this is only an assumption of mine, and I cannot promise my assumption to turn out being successful. But so far my advices were quite right, so that I suggest you do everything I proposed. Sending Arnold cables does not make sense as long as you cannot tell him that the trip to Japan will be sponsored from there [Germany]. At least he will then see that other places help as well.

In fact, do you already have your visa? I need to see an organization within the next few days anyway. I will once more discuss your case. You can count on me. I think about

Rosh Hashana, 1940

—

you and do everything in my power (you can tell due to the affidavit arrangements), but my limits are all too restricted unfortunately.

Do you happen to know any wealthy people here who can advance some money, so one is able to collect at least part of the sum? I know this question is somewhat childish, but you may think of somebody whom one could turn to.

This is all I can recommend to you today. I will remain being committed and will not forget all of you.

Luzie

———

As is apparent in this letter, Martha took Luzie's advice.

———

To: Arnold and Stephen Hatch, Albany, New York
From: Martha Harf, Cologne, Germany
Date: September 29, 1940

Dear Cousins,

I thank you for your letter by airmail of Aug. 12th, and reply to you as short as possible as I will not take your time for long.

I have heard that you, dear Arnold and dear Stephen, have made out the affidavits for Hechts in Shanghai and that you will take care of their coming over to USA, very, very generous of you.

By my cable of Aug. 19th you learned that your sent papers for Ruth and me are considered as sufficient by the American Consulate at Stuttgart. You may imagine how awfully happy we are about this. You are right: our heart is set on coming to America and making for ourselves a new life there. If I could speak to you only half an hour and explain all our troubles, you would surely understand our impatience to leave Germany as soon as possible.

We are able to pay our journeys from here to Yokohama or Kobe by our means, so that we beg you to be kind enough to pay the passage for us from one of this ports to New-York. If you would deposit the needed amount to a bank or Shipline-Agency and I should be exceedingly thankful to you. Without any such a certificate that the amount of the passage to USA is deposed, our visas are not granted. Before we are called to the American Consulate in Stuttgart, we must send this letter there. These regulations are new, perhaps according to the war conditions.

May I also let you know that Ruth is very talented in drawing, and that it is impossible here to find a teacher for her in this subject. That is a pity as this talent may be a good profession for her future.

Don't mind, dear Arnold, my repeating that there is no chance at all of making our living here, and it would be a very bad thing for us waiting for the end of the war. As to myself, I am still healthy enough and able to work hard. I suppose that after our coming to America we can speak about my husband's immigration.

Looking forward to a favorable reply, I remain, dear Arnold and dear Stephen,

Yours ever so thankfully

Martha

———

Rosh Hashana, 1940

—

To: Arnold Hatch, Albany, New York

From: Luzie Hatch, New York

Date: September 6, 1940

Dear Arnold:

I have received your letters of August 28th and September 3rd.

I noted what you said with regard to Aunt Martha's trip to this country, and we have informed her accordingly. I agree with you that it is a great undertaking to have people come via Siberia, but on the other hand, I know that at present many are doing this successfully.

As far as I know the fare until Yokohama can be paid for in German currency, and the Hilfsverein (the German committee) is said to have financed several trips from Germany to Yokohama for people without means. I, too, hope that the whole world situation will adjust itself soon making such difficulties a thing of the past.

Wishing you a pleasant weekend, I am, with much love

Yours, as ever,

Luzie

Three days later Arnold informed Luzie of his decision.

To: Luzie Hatch, New York
From: Arnold Hatch, Albany, New York
Date: September 9, 1940

Dear Luzie:

I have your letter and have written you about all that I have to say for the present about Martha and her daughter. You state that the Hilfsverein assists in financing some of these trips occasionally, but my experience as shown by what has just happened in the case of your family is that they cannot be depended upon to help at all. They make a lot of promises which are not kept.

I therefore place no reliance on any help that might be expected from that German committee, and I repeat again that Martha and her daughter will have to remain in Germany until conditions clear up. I hope that you have written them to this effect and made it clear.

As regards your own family, I would suggest that you look around and get a furnished room for them, near or with you in Forest Hills. As regards any other plans for them, those should wait until they arrive here. I want to see what physical condition they are in, whether they have even a nominal command of English, and a lot of other stuff before we even look into the matter of work for them.

With much love, I am

Yours, in haste,

Arnold

Rosh Hashana, 1940

Alfons remained persistent in his effort to emigrate to Latin America.

———

To: Luzie Hatch, New York
From: Alfons Isack, Essen, Germany
Date: September 17, 1940
Translated from the German

Dear Luzie!

Today I found time to answer your letter. I'm doing all right, and hope the same is true for you and Arnold, Herta, Edith, and Mann. I thank you, my dearest Luzie, for making these efforts in my matters, especially now that Arnold wants to help me out.

I went to the Benevolent Society and emigration is out of the question at the moment. As soon as I know where I can go, I'll let you and Arnold know. The main point is that Arnold will support me financially, in case I leave for South America. I assure him I will repay all of his expenditures. I have also registered to come to America, and I received a high number. If I were to wait for this number to be called, I would have to stay here for years to come.

Please let Arnold read this letter. I don't want to forget to wish you, Arnold and his family, a "Happy New Year." Please don't write anymore to Aunt Lina and Uncle Max. They're saying horrible things about you, and because of that, I'll be mad at them forever. They've also talked about me behind my back, and I'm done with them. In case you are writing to your parents, please give them my regards.

September 1939–October 1941

—

200

I'll finish writing now since I also want to write to Aunt Jula and Käte. I want to hug and kiss you and all of your loved ones,

your cousin Alfons

Please write soon.

———

———

To: Alfons Isack, Essen, Germany

From: Luzie Hatch, New York

Date: November 24, 1940

Translated from the German

Dear Alfons, my dears [other cousins]:

To you dear Alfons, I can only keep repeating that unfortunately at the moment I don't see any possibility for you to realize your plans, as you have also written yourself. In any case, of course I will do everything I can to help you when the time comes.

In any case, I recommend that you 1) continue to keep me informed ... 2) also write to Arnold every now and then, even when you don't have much to report, so that you will stay fresh in his memory.

As I have already written to you many times, I see him rarely, but when I do see him once every few months, I always mention you. So, as I said, maintain the communication, and hopefully we will find a solution soon.

From the signatures below you will see that my parents and Rolf have now arrived, thank goodness. They arrived in early October and are in fairly good health.

From me personally I can tell you that I am in good

Rosh Hashana, 1940

—

health and hope to get through the winter well this time, so as not to get sick again as I was last year. I am working hard and happy to have the same position.

For the next letter you do not need to enclose reply coupons. I will answer you anyway, and you should save money.

So, my dears, I look forward to hearing from you soon. Stay healthy, and may the New Year bring you what you desire.

With all my love and kisses for you all,

Luzie

———

Aunt Paula Steinberg was not shy about voicing her keen disappointment in her niece. Caught in a whirlwind of torment and change, she had few to turn to for support. Her husband, Hermann, had been killed in World War I, and all three of her children had gone to Palestine. She was alone and frightened, and her anger at Luzie for not writing more often was not surprising.

———

To: Luzie Hatch, New York
From: Paula Steinberg, Dortmund, Germany
Date: September 18, 1940
Translated from the German

My dear devil Luzie!

I could not believe my eyes when approximately three weeks ago your letter of 08/08 arrived here! I totally gave up on you, and was no longer counting on a sign of life from you. Only <u>perhaps</u> it would have been your responsibility to answer my letter of 05/28 to Erna or Hilde.

But as mentioned, love can't be forced, and nor can letter writing!

Considering that, perhaps you can understand how I am feeling. There are no excuses, no matter how busy you may have been. If the situation was reversed, dear Luzie, I certainly would have acted differently, and would not have kept you waiting for so long. But all of you on the outside no longer have a real appreciation for those of us who are left behind, and I don't think I deserved that from you!

With time one becomes bitter, dear Luzie. All that I have left, my children and my grandchildren, are far away. How often must they too think of me and worry about me! I hope they are all healthy, and I was very happy to hear that you are also in good health again and that you have returned to your former weight. Thank God I am also doing quite well so far, only so much is missing!!

Unfortunately, Uncle Max was very sick with pneumonia, and he is having so much trouble recovering. It is generally very hard for them too, and they have little chance of leaving . . .

I have gotten myself a number on the waiting list for the U.S.A. as a last resort. I have #44184, but surely I won't put it to use, because who would be my guarantor! There is little relying on friends and relatives, dear child; one realizes that time and again. And I don't want to be in a foreign country without my children. I will just stay here until I can join them. And if there is a God, hopefully he will grant me that blessing.

I wish you all the very best for the holiday season, how about a nice man that I wish for you in the coming year? It

Rosh Hashana, 1940

—

is about time now, my dear child, or should you not want that?

For the time being, I am not permitted to send a picture of myself. But when I am so disposed, I will have myself photographed and send one along to you at the earliest opportunity.

Farewell, and keep your word about writing!

Reply coupon enclosed. I send you my love and kisses.

Your Aunt Paula, Lots of love from Uncle Jakob

———

Aunt Paula, for understandable reasons, was becoming increasingly bitter and depressed. And Luzie's cousin Dora was faring no better.

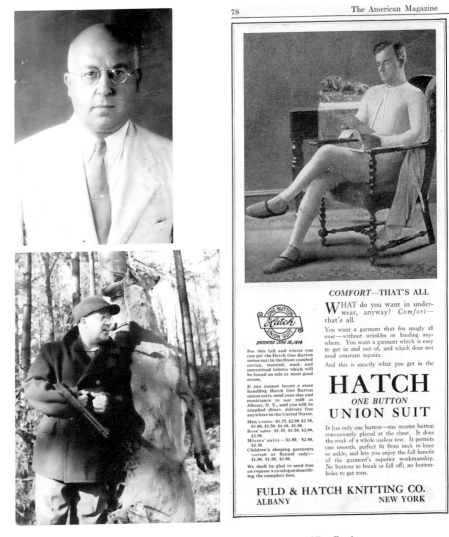

Above, left Portrait of Arnold Hatch, Luzie's cousin. Courtesy of Pat Roth.

Right From *American Magazine*, ca. 1920s.

Below, left Arnold Hatch, Luzie's cousin. Courtesy of Pat Roth.

Top Edwin Hecht, Luzie's father, and Ralph, her half-brother, ca. 1930. Courtesy of Ralph Hatch.

Bottom Inge Friedländer, sixth from right, and Ralph Hatch, second from right, in front of their Berlin apartment, ca. 1928. Courtesy of Ralph Hatch.

Top left Back row, left to right: Leo Rosenfeld, Dora Hecht, Marta Hecht. Courtesy of Michael Merose.

Top right Paula Steinberg, Luzie's aunt. Courtesy of Dan Mendels.

Bottom German Jews deported from Mannheim, Germany, to Vichy France, October 1940. Courtesy of Hauptstaatsarchiv Stuttgart.

Hunger—Camp de Gurs, by Karl Borg. Courtesy of Archiv für Zeitgeschichte, Zurich.

Above Luzie Hatch, ca. 1950s.

Below Luzie Hatch with friends at the World Trade Center, ca. 1970s.

Above, top Front, far left, Ralph Hecht, Luzie's half-brother. Back, far left, Edwin Hecht, Luzie's father, ca. 1929. Courtesy of Ralph Hatch.

Above, bottom Front, Edwin Hecht, Luzie's father. Back, third from right, Ralph Hecht, Luzie's half-brother, ca. 1929. Courtesy of Ralph Hatch.

Above, top Luzie with her brother, Ralph, ca. 1931. Courtesy of Ralph Hatch.

Above, bottom Left to right, sisters Marta Rosenfeld and Dora Hecht. Courtesy of Michael Merose.

Norddeutscher Lloyd
Bremen

An die

nichtarischen Passagiere der Touristen-Klasse!

Ich bitte die nichtarischen deutschen Passagiere höflichst, unter Rücksichtnahme auf die bekannte Einstellung der deutschen arischen Passagiere, sich außer des Speisesaals, nur des an Steuerbord gelegenen Rauchzimmers bedienen zu wollen.

Ferner bitte ich die nichtarischen Passagiere, das Schwimmbad nur von 9 bis 15 Uhr täglich zu benutzen.

O. PREHN Kapitän

The Hecht family's departure from Germany: message from captain of the *Potsdam*, March 3, 1939. Courtesy of Ralph Hatch. Translation: "Norddeutscher Lloyd Bremen / (Northern German Lloyd Bremen) Commando / D. Potsdam / March 3, 1939 / To the non-Aryan passengers in Tourist Class! / Out of consideration for the Aryan passengers' well-known disposition, I kindly request that, apart from the dining hall, non-Aryan passengers only use the smoking room on starboard. / Moreover, I request that non-Aryan passengers use the swimming pool only from 9 a.m. to 3 p.m. daily. / O. Prehn Captain"

12

Deportation to Gurs

ILOT K

"My stay here is now soon coming to an end. The thought of falling prey to the Jewish social services depresses me very much, but what can I do? I am just old, sick, destitute, and homeless." These were Dora's words to Luzie in September 1940. She had learned for certain that she would no longer have any access to her brother-in-law Leopold's estate. As disturbing as this news was, Dora's financial distress would soon be displaced by a matter of even greater concern.

Each day, in the office at the American Jewish Committee, Luzie could read news from around the world via the daily wires of the Jewish Telegraphic Agency. On October 29th, the JTA wire stunned her. "Thousands are being shipped out of Baden and the Palatinate under orders of the Gestapo and Nazi officials."[1] Most certainly she hoped for the best, but she must have been plagued by nagging suspicions that Dora had been placed on a transport out of Baden-Baden. How likely would it have been that an elderly and ill woman, largely homebound, would have escaped the morning knock at her door? Finally, in November, Luzie had an answer. A cable arrived with the news that Dora was in an internment camp in Vichy France.

The Vichy Transports

France, which had battled the Germans for four long years in World War I, now collapsed in a mere six weeks, surrendering on June 22, 1940. The collaborationist Vichy regime was established, with the Germans occupying northern France and the south remaining unoccupied. With more than a bit of sarcasm, a State Department staffer cabled Washington: "The first 'benefit' for France in the new Franco-German collaboration policy has been the arrival of between four and five thousand German-Jews from the Palatinate."[2]

On October 22, 1940, the Jews of Baden and Saarplatz were arrested for deportation to Vichy France. Although Dora's letters do not describe the deportation itself, Hilde Übelacker, then Hilde Besag, a deportee on the Vichy transports who still lives in her hometown of Baden-Baden, was able to give me a first-person account of that harrowing journey in an interview at her home. Sitting in her living room with the windows swung wide open, we could gaze out at what she warmly called "my valley." I could not help but think of the early Baden travel guides I had read, with their praise of a land "delightful beyond measure." In this relaxing and inviting setting, she recalled the morning of their arrest.

Hilde Besag, then nineteen years old, was at the breakfast table with her three sisters, mother, and grandmother, fortifying herself for another routine day of farmwork. The family members were not paid laborers but volunteers helping a neighboring farmer who was struggling because of the labor shortage caused by the war. The warm relationship the Besags had with the local farmer would be cut off by a ringing doorbell.

The Nazi officers at the doorstep delivered a chilling message. "You have to leave, and you won't come back to Germany." The instructions were terse and simple. Each family member could take fifty kilograms of luggage. The officers would return in one hour to pick them up.[3]

What happened at the Besag household was repeated throughout the Baden and Saar-Palatinate region. Starting at 6:00 a.m., Nazis officers knocked on the doors of all Jewish households, repeating the same orders. Yet in one respect, the Besags' experience may not have paralleled that of Baden's Jews. Hilde notes that her family had had absolutely no warning of their impending deportation. "Shock" is the word she repeated again and again.

This is because by birth, conviction, and upbringing, Hilde and her family were Protestants. Hilde's paternal grandparents, the Besags, had left the Jewish community though stopped short of converting to Christianity, and her maternal grandparents had converted to Protestantism. Yet in the Nazi racial prism, whereby genetics and blood were central, a Jewish identity was not so easily erased.

Lacking contact with Jewish families or institutions, the Besags had no way of knowing that the day before, October 21, 1940, Jewish workers in the districts of Baden and the Saar-Palatinate were instructed not to report to work the next day. As a pensioner, Dora would not have received this order, but as a member of the Jewish community, she might have learned of it. Although those who heard this news could not have known what exactly would transpire the next morning, they must have gone to bed with deep anxiety.

On hearing the deportation order, Hilde's first thought was to go into hiding, but realizing that this was not possible, she hurriedly packed her belongings. Meanwhile, one of her sisters went to the nearby farm to tell the farmer that they would not be coming to work. Stunned by the news, the farmer returned to the Besag home with Hilde's sister.

As they had promised, the Nazis returned an hour later. Hilde, her three sisters, mother, and seventy-two-year-old grandmother all boarded the "lorry." "Why are you doing this?" the farmer asked, tears running down his face. Trying to save the family, he raised the issue of simple economic practicality. "Who will work my farm?" he asked. "He was simply overwhelmed with despair for what was being done to us," Hilde recalls. "It was the first time I had ever seen a man cry."[4]

As the truck ambled down the hill toward town, one deportee asked the question that was terrifying so many: "Are we going to Poland?" Hilde recalls, "We knew the East was terrible. The officer answered, 'No, you are going west.' We felt a little better knowing that we were going west."[5]

They were taken to the town hall, the collection point for Baden-Baden's Jews. Seeing the steady stream of Jewish deportees arrive, one after another, Hilde was struck by the extensive nature of the action. In response to my question whether they slept at the town hall that night, she replied, "If you could sleep."[6]

The physical expulsion of the Jews and the subsequent purification and preservation of Aryan society was not the only benefit of the deportation for the Nazis. There was another bounty: the confiscation of Jewish property. As always, the act of thievery was clothed in legal trappings. The official who filed a report on the deportation with the foreign office noted: "Since in many cases the expatriation was done unlawfully, meaning that a fee for leaving the Reich was not properly paid, we have frozen all assets."[7]

Dora, like all Jews, was required to sign a power of attorney transferring her belongings, which included the recent funds Arnold had wired to her, to the German government.

Gauleiters Josef Bürckel and Josef Wagner, the Nazi regional leaders who ordered the deportation, had instructed subordinates working on the action that "all members of the Jewish race have to be deported as long as they can travel."[8] A memo entitled "Report on the Deportation of German Jews to Southern France," filed with the Nazi Foreign Office one week after the deportation, explained just how thoroughly these orders had been followed.

Age or sex was not to be taken into consideration. We made some exceptions when it came to mixed marriages. Even men who had been fighting for Germany in World War I and their officers had to be deported. The old age homes in Mannheim, Karlsruhe, Ludwigshafen, and so forth were emptied out. Men and women who were unable to walk were put on stretchers and put on trains. The oldest deportee was a 97-year-old man from Karlsruhe.[9]

After the deportation, the Baden-Palatinate region was almost completely Judenrein, "cleared of Jews." Only a handful remained. Twenty-six Jews avoided deportation because they had Christian spouses. Fifteen Jews were deemed unable to travel, apparently even on a stretcher. Five more were allowed to stay and tend to these invalids. Others avoided deportation through their own actions. Two fled the area, while others decided on another means, suicide.[10] On the morning of the transport, the Nazis recorded eight suicides in Mannheim and three in Karlsruhe.[11]

Of the more than 6,504 Jews who were rounded up and deported from the area, 116 deportees came from Dora's town of Baden-Baden. An examination of the Nazi roster for the town reveals that it was largely a deportation of older women: 66 percent were female and 58 percent were sixty or older.[12] The youngest deportee from the town was Manfred Kirschner. As a twelve-year-old, not fully comprehending what was unfolding, his reaction differed from Hilde's, being more one of surprise than shock. Lessening the tension of the day was the fact that his family remained intact. "We always did everything together as a family," he explains, "whether it was taking an excursion or playing music or whatever, working around the house in the garden ... So as long as I went with my family I was not that shocked. It was just we were going somewhere else and you really didn't know where."[13]

Pleased that the action had gone so smoothly, Reinhard Heydrich, head of the Reich Central Security Office, filed his report. The deportation "took place in all localities of Baden and the Palatinate without friction and without incidents. The operation itself was scarcely realized by the population."[14] Author Angelika Schindler's work on the Jews of Baden-Baden supports Heydrich's claim of a stealthy operation, at least in this one town. When conducting her research, she found few residents willing to speak of the transport, but those who would repeatedly said they were unaware of the action. "First of all," Schindler explains, "there were only about 120 Jews in Baden. And the town hall, the collection point, was not in the center of town but on the outskirts ... And it's a terrible thing to say, but by this time the Jews were so isolated that people were used to them not being a part of their lives."[15]

It is important to note that the Nazis' Jewish policy at this point was not extermination but emigration enacted through discrimination and terror. However, given that the outside world shut its doors and refused to cooperate, they not surprisingly cast their eyes on nearby Vichy France. Here was a convenient dumping ground for at least some of Germany's remaining Jews.[16] And so, at the end of October 1940, twelve sealed train cars, filled with Jewish expellees, rolled out of Germany. The trains would pass through Freiburg, Mühlhausen, Belfort, Besançon, Lyon, Avignon, and Toulouse. The trains rolled on and made a stop in Lourdes, where Hilde thought, "So far south? We still had no idea where we were going."[17]

Given no forewarning of the arrival of these German Jews, the Vichy government reacted with anger and alarm. Initially, the French refused to accept the trains, declaring that this action was a violation of the armistice. Hilde remembers a very long holdup at the frontier to Vichy France. Determined that all stay on board, the officials blared a warning over the loudspeaker: "If you leave the train, you will be shot." "We knew that this was true," she commented, "so you didn't do it."[18]

The deportees endured a long and arduous two-day train trip. Most had brought a bit of food with them—bread, cookies, apples, and sausage; these meager provisions would be their only sustenance apart from the soup dispensed by the Nazis. Hilde Übelacker has no recollection of any discussions that took place during this forty-eight-hour ordeal, only the memory of being completely stunned. During this journey, some on board chose to end their lives.

In the end, Vichy France acceded to Nazi demands and received the deportees. On the night of October 24, the trains arrived during a rainstorm at the town of Oloron-Sainte-Marie. On disembarking, they were transferred to trucks for the six-mile drive to the internment camp at Gurs.

Internment at Gurs

The camp sat at the foot of the Pyrenees, in southwestern France, fifty miles from the Spanish border. Gurs had been hastily constructed in 1939 as an internment center for refugees of the Spanish Civil War. Its original inhabitants, a mix of female enemy aliens and their children, Spaniards, and French political dissenters, had totaled 15,793; this had dwindled to a population of slightly more than 3,000 by the time of Dora's arrival.[19]

The commandant at Gurs had no idea why German Jews had been sent there, nor was he prepared for them.[20] He had been given a mere three hours' advance notice to ready the facility for their arrival, an action that would more than triple the camp population. Records indicate that the Nazis were aware of the commandant's dilemma. "There won't be enough appropriate housing or food for the often older deportees," wrote an official who worked on the transport. "As far as we know," he continued, "the French government contemplates sending them to Madagascar as soon as the ocean route opens up."[21]

Gurs measured approximately 1,500 yards in length and 200 in width. A main road ran the full length of the camp, bisecting it into sections that were then subdivided into *ilots,* or blocks, each containing approximately twenty barracks. Barbed wire surrounded every ilot, and a sentry stood guard at the ilot's only exit. The camp had been built on marshy ground, a fact that would create nightmarish conditions when the rains came. "Outside, between barracks and barbed wire," commented one aid worker, "there is mud—deep mud, and winter and spring in these regions bring rain and more rain, and the mud grows ever worse."[22] The sludge that engulfed the camp was far more than an inconvenience that soiled one's shoes and clothing. Camp survivor Hanne Hirsch Liebmann notes that the first death in her group was not from disease or starvation but from the Gurs mud. "When it rained, you sank into the clay up to your knees. The first persons we lost . . . choked to death in the mud. She went at night to the latrine. She fell. She could not extricate herself and she died."[23]

Manfred Kirschner remembers that on disembarking from the train at Gurs, his family was instructed to leave their luggage, with the promise that it would be brought to them later. "My father said 'Under no circumstances. Take everything you can with you. You can't trust anybody from now on.' And he was right. After a couple of days they brought the luggage and left it right outside the barbed wire fence so you could see your luggage melt away in the rain. And they left it there until it was just garbage."[24]

The conditions facing the arriving Jewish internees were also documented by a survivor from Mannheim, Germany, who left a telling description: "Soaked by rain, shivering with cold, exhausted by the long voyage, the flock was pushed in indescribable disorder into empty barracks, without benches, without straw, without mattresses. Collapsed against their bundles many old people spent the night."[25] Dora Hecht had been assigned to barrack 9, Ilot K.

Her first letter from Gurs, a direct appeal to Arnold for two hundred dollars, arrived in Albany at the beginning of December. She wrote that with this sum, she could buy her freedom from Gurs. Arnold had many and varied suspicions; of the Vichy French, of the letter, and even of the American Jewish Committee, which he calls a "propaganda agency."

—

To: Luzie Hatch, New York
From: Arnold Hatch, Albany, New York
Date: December 6, 1940

Dear Luzie:

Yesterday I received the enclosed airmail letter from Dora, written from the camp in which she supposedly is— that is, I think she wrote it, although I am not too familiar with her handwriting. I have had the letter translated, and note her statement that if we will cable her $200.00 over there, she will be released from the camp. I also note that the letter does not state what she will do, if released, where she will go, or what is to happen to her then.

The party who translated this letter for me and who has had a lot of experience in these matters looks upon this letter with great suspicion. He seems to think that the sending of this money will do no good and is of the opinion that Dora was, perhaps, forced to write it. In particular, he called my attention to the postscript on the letter in which Dora asked for various things to be sent her including a summer hat. This party seems to think that the request for a summer hat wanted by a woman during the winter in the Pyrenees Mountains is so outrageously ridiculous that it is her way of telling me that this whole letter means nothing.

Now, I want to do anything possible for this old lady, but I hate the idea of cabling over money which will not do her any good, which she will not, perhaps, even receive, and which will not accomplish the desired result. You know, of course, that I have already sent her some money a day or so after she wrote this letter on which I have not had any acknowledgement from either the bankers or Dora.

You might give me your opinion of all this, and if you can submit the letter to one of the New York City agencies dealing in these matters, I should like their opinion also. I do not necessarily mean your own outfit which is a propaganda agency; but rather one of the others.

With much love to you and all your family, I am

Yours as ever, Arnold

———

Luzie tried to explain as much as she could to Arnold.

———

To: Arnold Hatch, Albany, New York
From: Luzie Hatch, New York
Date: December 10, 1940

Dear Arnold:

I received your letter of December 6 and noted all you say about Dora's airmail letter. Her letter seems to be genuine. The way the envelope was closed, or rather half open, seems to indicate that camp authorities read the letters before letting them pass; obviously the people [Gurs's internees] are encouraged to give the most gloomy descriptions in order to receive foreign exchange. This is contrary to what I experienced in Germany, where the Nazis strictly forbade even the slightest description of critical conditions.

Dora may possibly have requested the $200, either because of pressure by the camp officials, or with the intention of impressing them with the fact that in time a big sum of dollars may be expected, in the hope of thus alleviating her position.

At this time it is considered inadvisable to send large sums of money. No more than $5 or $10 should be sent at any one time and more could be promised. Most probably, the money only gets into the hands of Fascist circles—whether Nazis or French does not make any difference—and helps, together with many other things, to lengthen the war in favor of the Germans.

There is a rule here prohibiting the sending of large amounts, but if one can proof that smaller amounts have been remitted regularly for some time, permission will be given to continue to do so. Your bank will certainly be informed about this.

Incidentally, the American Jewish Committee is not a propaganda outfit. It has to do with propaganda only insofar as it believes in the necessity of "exposing" hostile or subversive propaganda. The work of the Committee is all-embracing, and while many immigration and refugee questions are referred to other organizations (some of which the Committee was instrumental in establishing), the Committee is very much concerned with these problems, too.

Hoping that you are fine and that I will have the pleasure of seeing you soon again, I am, with much love,

Yours, as ever,

Luzie

———

Next, Luzie wrote to Dora trying to obtain more information.

To: Dora Hecht, Camp Gurs, France
From: Luzie Hatch, New York
Date: Undated
Translated from the German

Dear Dora:

Arnold received your airmail letter of November 6 after the usual delay. He studied it with greatest interest and has thought over your situation from every angle. The results of his deliberations are the following:

Arnold is still waiting for an acknowledgment of the approximately 2,200 francs sent to you there in November. He is still wondering whether you have received the money and would like to know this before he does anything further.

How are the $200.00 requested for your release to be spent? Where will you go and what are you going to do? Is there any place for you to go to if you are released from the camp? Evidently, it seems not to be realized over there that it is not so easy to send $200.00 from here across the ocean, even if after some efforts such an amount can be raised. There are many formalities to be fulfilled and a lot of regulations have to be observed.

Arnold asks you to reply to the above questions by airmail. The more official details given, the more Arnold will be induced to help. As outlined before, he is perfectly willing to help if in doing so he can be of constructive help.

But it should not be forgotten that he has a lot of obligations himself.

To send clothing is also not so easy, but we are trying to find out the best way to do it and hope that something can be accomplished in this direction, too.

I hope, dear Dora, that all this shows that we are much concerned about you. I know empty words do not help much, but perhaps the assurance of our interest and readiness to help give you a little hope for a better future. How is your health, can you do anything for yourself?

With best wishes from Arnold and myself, I am,

Yours

Luzie

———

Arnold and Luzie often discussed the complications of sending money to Dora. The US Treasury Department permitted American banks to transmit up to fifty dollars a month to an individual in Vichy France, provided that the sender met two criteria. First, the individual sending the funds had to have resided in the United States for a year or more. Second, the sender had to show that he or she had been granting financial aid to the intended recipient since October 1939. Fortunately, Arnold met both of these conditions.[26] Yet Dora was not requesting fifty dollars but two hundred, a transaction that would have required special permission.

For those in the United States trying to assist relatives abroad, tasks were never simple. Even an act that would normally be considered uncomplicated—cabling money to a relative abroad—was freighted with bureaucratic regulations.

Back in 1940, Arnold had few hard facts about life at Gurs. He could only proceed on his instincts, which told him that that the cabling of two hundred dollars would not buy Dora's release. But was he correct or just hardhearted and mistaken?

Relief workers at the internment camps in Vichy France often discussed the subject of release. Gaining release from the camps was possible, but the process was difficult and therefore rare.

As one HICEM relief worker stated, "Each case of liberation, even if that person wants to reside in a village quite near the camp, is the object of a special examination of the central power ... These liberations are given only in very exceptional cases and after very long and very difficult negotiations."[27] This relief worker penned his analysis in December 1940, very close to the date that Dora had written that for a price of two hundred dollars, she would be able to leave Gurs.

Just two months later, Joseph J. Schwartz, vice chairman of the American Joint Distribution Committee's Lisbon office, addressed the question of liberation from Gurs in a letter to the New York office.

> One must have permission from a prefecture to establish residence before release will be agreed to by the camp authorities. The prefectures, as a rule, do not give these permits of residence because they are not interested in the amount of money one possesses but in keeping out as many mouths as possible ... It is the problem of food, rather than money, which is complicating the release of camp internees.[28]

Of the 21,794 people interned at Gurs from October 24, 1940, to November 1943, only 1,710 were released to either live in France or return to their homeland. In addition, 1,940 internees were released after compiling the necessary emigration papers; unfortunately, 30 percent of these individuals failed to emigrate and were returned to Gurs. Finally, 755 camp prisoners escaped.[29] So, in fact, back in 1940, Arnold's hunch was probably accurate.

———

To: Luzie Hatch, New York
From: Arnold Hatch, Albany, New York
Date: December 11, 1940

Dear Luzie:

I have your letter of December 10th and note carefully what you say. Last month, as you know, I sent the proceeds of $50.00 to Dora, which came to about 2200 French francs, but there has been no acknowledgement of the money so far. I am still wondering whether she has gotten the money or will be allowed to enjoy it.

I would prefer not to send anything more until I find out somehow or other if Dora is receiving the money already sent. If you write her your letter, I would suggest that you ask her to send a reply by airmail because ordinary letter transportation takes too long.

In brief, I am perfectly willing to do anything I can for this unfortunate woman, but I hate the idea of sending over money which benefits someone else. If you will handle this for me, I will appreciate it.

Yours as ever,
Arnold

———

To: Arnold Hatch, Albany, New York
From: Luzie Hatch, New York
Date: December 17, 1940

Dear Arnold:

I am sure that Dora understands that you are willing to help, but that for educational reasons it must be pointed out that it is not so easy to raise any given amount, otherwise the authorities take advantage of relatives over here.

I think that you and Rose [Arnold's wife] would not mind helping Dora out with some clothing. I called up the Red Cross and they told me there is no guarantee that those parcels arrive. They do not handle such cases but only send parcels to prisoners of war. People who send such packages do so at their own risk. I shall follow this up with other organizations and shall inform you of the results.

I think this is all I can do at the present time. You know I am always willing to carry out your wishes and am awaiting your further instructions.

We are getting along fine. Rolf—who has changed his name to Ralph in the meantime enjoyed the lunch with Arnie very much. My mother is doing some homework. She is putting leather pieces together in the shape of novelty dogs, horses, etc. It is much work and is very poorly paid, but at least she earns a few dollars.

Now I am concerned with what my father will do after his return next week from Wilkes Barre, where he went following your advice to take it easy for some time in order to get stronger. Of course, we shall try very hard to find work

Deportation to Gurs

for him. After the great generosity which you have shown us in the past I hesitate to trouble you about our current troubles, but we would appreciate so much getting your advice on this problem.

With much love to you, I am

Luzie

———

This following note from Marta Rosenfeld to her sister, Dora, probably a birthday greeting since both were born in December, is only a fragment, yet these few lines reveal the deep bond between the two sisters.[30]

———

To: Dora Hecht, Camps Gurs, Vichy France

From: Marta Rosenfeld, Palestine

Date: December 1940

Translated from the German

... since the two cannot come together, to be united once again. In the meantime we cannot do anything else but to bear up and not jeopardize our health even more by dark thoughts.

So for today, dear Dorle, our warmest regards to you, take care and keep well and let us soon rejoice in good news from you.

Your loving Marta, who is attaching by her own hand ... We [Marta and her husband, Leopold] are sending from our hearts a kiss.

———

September 1939–October 1941

—

222

Cousin Dora's situation was getting more complicated, and Arnold's misgivings continued to grow in turn.

———

To: Luzie Hatch, New York
From: Arnold Hatch, Albany, New York
Date: January 13, 1941

Dear Luzie:

I just received the enclosed letter supposed to come from Dora, and I should like your opinion of it.

I must admit that I view this letter with the gravest suspicion. In all the years I have never had any letter from Dora before written in English, and I am of the opinion that she cannot write English. If it were necessary for someone else to write this letter for her, I do not know why she could not mention that fact. It is obvious that a great many parts of the body of this letter were not written by her, if any of it was. The only thing that looks genuine is the signature, which could easily enough be duplicated.

On top of all that, I have never received any letter out of Germany in recent times which so boldly told the misery and shortage and suffering experienced, and I do not believe that she would be allowed to write any such letter except for the fact that this is a bold effort to get more money. I am also extremely dubious that she is getting the benefit of what we send.

As stated above, you might read this over and if you like, have someone else in your organization pass on it, and let me know your views.

I hate to keep sending money over there which will benefit the Nazis and not her. I am more than a little suspicious of this whole thing. They may not give her much to eat, but they are certainly giving her a marvelous education if in the six weeks that she is in the camp, she could learn to write an English letter like this.

I hope that you and your family are well, and one of these days if I get out from under all the troubles which beset me at this time, I hope to have an opportunity of seeing you all again. With much love, I am

Yours as ever,

Arnold

———

———

To: Arnold Hatch, Albany, NY, USA
From: Luzie Hatch, New York, NY, USA
Date: January 26, 1941

Dear Arnold:

I studied the questions of your letter of January 17th very carefully. In my opinion Dora's letter is not to be viewed with suspicion. Obviously, she got the assistance of somebody familiar with the English language and might not have mentioned the fact because it did not seem important to her. Although in some cases there may be cause for suspicion, I believe that the letter expresses her own thoughts and feelings. American organizations and private persons are receiving similar descriptions. These correspond with an article of today's *New York Times* which I am enclosing, although you may have read it in the meantime.

Various organizations are now trying to help the unfortunate inhabitants of this Camp.

Dora lives in unoccupied France, and her letters are not subject to criticism by German censors; thus she is in a position to write about her miserable situation. The money you sent her in November has evidently been paid to her and has helped her a lot. I heard that in some cases people have been released from camp after receiving a certain sum as Dora mentioned in her letter. However, the prerequisite for getting a person out of France is an affidavit. Maybe the French Fascist circles might profit in some way from money sent from America, but, on the other hand, it evidently helps to relieve the misery of the unhappy people in this Camp.

I can imagine that there is a lot of trouble with which you have to fight at present, and I am looking forward to the time when you can give me an opportunity to see you again.

Yours, as ever,

Luzie

———

Luzie tried to allay Arnold's suspicions, arguing that the money he sent her had not lined the pockets of a camp official but had actually reached Dora and eased her misery. Unfortunately, Dora's letter, in which, in Arnold's words, she so "boldly" described the misery and suffering at Gurs, has been lost.

But many others also wrote "boldly" of life at Gurs, and their recollections have not been misplaced or discarded. Workers from numerous relief organizations have left volumes of paperwork detailing all aspects of camp life. It would have been difficult for Dora to exaggerate the torment of her days at Gurs.

The Emergency Rescue Committee in New York City received this description from one of its contacts in France: "The camp of Gurs is composed of thin wooden barracks of which furnish no protection against the rain . . . Sixty people are crowded in each barrack, one straw sack near the other; there are no chairs, no tables, no place to eat—each man's existence is confined to his straw sack."[31]

Written in the early winter of 1941, the report went on to note, "The mortality rate has increased enormously—several deaths each day, particularly among people recently sent over from Germany. Children born in this camp have to be wrapped in newspapers because there is no linen; old men and women simply die of cold and hunger."[32] Hilde Übelacker remembers how, in that first winter at Gurs, she would stand at the barrack door each morning and count the coffins being taken out of the camp.[33]

Manfred Kirschner, the youngest Baden-Baden deportee, recalls holding hands with many dying internees. "If you were not in agony or tortured of anything, people slip away rather peacefully." But as he explains, this was not always the case. "The problem was that many people had diarrhea and that really empties you out and can be painful. People tried to get coal dust [to eat]. Coal dust absorbs moisture and would clog you up a little bit because people would literally bleed to death going to the toilet." In his time at Gurs, this teenager would come to "accept death as part of life."[34]

Baden-Baden resident Oskar Wolf kept a diary of his time at Gurs for the children "Werner and Erich, to remember our difficult, difficult times."[35] Page after page detail not only specific daily events and his thoughts but a count of the staggering death rate.

September 1939–October 1941

—

Monday, December 2, 1940: Today again we had 12 funerals; Frau Wildberg's was one of them. This mass death was just horrible to see! The weather was cold a lot of frost. Without heat we were sitting and walking around in our almost pitch-black barrack. This was an unworthy existence.

Tuesday, December 3, 1940: Today we had 14 funerals. Our barrack has now been insulated to protect us against the cold. Because of the insulation, it was even darker inside.

Wednesday, December 4: Today we had 17 funerals.[36]

Driving the increased mortality rate, in large part, was the undernourishment of the internees. "Three months of Yom Kippur" is how one internee described his time at Gurs.[37] The daily ration at Gurs was 1,200 calories at the end of 1940; in 1941, it totaled only 1,000 calories. Although specific living conditions varied from camp to camp, the one constant, explained a French doctor in early 1941, was the insufficient food supply. "All the interned show signs of undernourishment, characterized by marked loss of weight, anemia of the mucous membranes, a pallor particularly marked among the women and children, more and more of whom have a waxy appearance."[38]

Both Manfred Kirschner and Hilde Übelacker remember daily meals limited to a little bread, coffee or "brown water," as Hilde described it, and watery soup with a few pieces of root vegetables. As Hilde notes, it was a diet with "no fat, no sugar, no meat."[39] At mid-day, Manfred and two or three other younger men who were still in relatively good health would pick up a huge pot of watery soup from the kitchen and trudge through the deep mud to bring it back to the barracks. The chore was done with great care. A bad burn in Gurs, where medical supplies were limited and the poor sanitary conditions were ripe for disease, could be life threatening. And if they were to stumble, sending the broth streaming into the mud, there would be no replacement meal. Those waiting at the barracks, hungry and anxious, would surely have exploded in anger.

In January 1941, the American Friends Service Committee began providing 1,300 internees at Gurs with 100 grams, slightly less than one quarter of a pound, of supplementary food.[40] Luzie's cousin Dora was probably chosen for this program, since the committee's report states that approximately 75 percent of those receiving the supplement were over fifty years of age and the greater part were German Jews from Baden and the Palatinate. While surely Dora must have welcomed this extra bit of food, if indeed she received it, she still was subsisting on an inadequate diet.

Malnourishment and famine were not the only factors contributing to sickness and death at Gurs. The hygienic conditions were terrible. To reach the outhouses, located over an open row of exposed garbage cans, internees had to walk between fifty and a hundred yards, braving the cold and the mud. Further hazards were open water pipes holding stagnant water, a breeding ground for disease.

Under these conditions, vermin such as rats and lice quickly became a problem. When a new, deadly illness that caused an inflammation of the brain appeared, aid workers noticed that the afflicted showed a particularly heavy infection of lice. In response, the Unitarian Service Committee purchased tubs for boiling underwear and irons, which noticeably lessened the problem.[41]

While the American Joint Distribution Committee, American Friends Service Committee, Unitarian Service Committee, Secours

Suisse, American ORT Society, Oeuvre de Secours aux Enfants (a French child welfare agency), the Committee for Aid to Gurs in Buenos Aires, and others worked to alleviate the suffering of internees at all the camps, the problem was simply too enormous even for their combined efforts.

Thus, even though internees benefited from the presence of these relief agencies, the aid of family and friends on the outside remained essential. Financial gifts from abroad allowed internees to go to the camp canteen, a store where one could purchase extra food. The term *canteen* should not conjure up an image of a grocery store with stocked shelves and a full assortment of products. Food was in short supply throughout the region, and the offerings on the canteen's shelves were limited. Still, whatever could be bought was an important supplement to the internees' meager rations.

Outside assistance came not only in the form of financial gifts but also as food parcels. For an inmate at Gurs, as Dora explains, a basic package of crackers and cake was a joyful event.

———

To: Luzie Hatch, New York
From: Dora Hecht, Camp Gurs, Vichy France
Date: February 25, 1941
Translated from the German

The exodus has already begun
The barracks are slowly emptying out.
Camp de Guerre
My dear Luzie!

Today I want to finally answer your kind letter, that made me <u>very</u> happy, and for which I thank you with all my heart, as well as dear Arnold, at whose request you wrote to me. As of today, I have not yet received the sum of money that I had been advised of. And in the meantime, I took out a little loan from the son of my cousin in Wiesbaden. What good fortune that I have someone here to assist me.

Our stay here is coming to an end. It is possible that we may move to a new camp in as little as eight days. Probably in Noé, near Toulouse. There, we will find better accommodations, which we are all very happy about; even the climate there is supposed to be better.

Here we have had so much rain since our arrival, and the roads are often barely passable—but you have to leave the barracks in wind and weather to use the water closet, which is very unpleasant, particularly at night. There we will have brighter rooms, and a table and chair where we can take our meals.

Last week, when a large number of American letters were delivered to the barracks, I was also one of the lucky people to receive one (from Arnold). But in the evening, I learned that a family from the Pfalz was taken to another camp. This was a hard blow for me and I was deeply saddened because these people took care of me better than anyone else could have. The dear Lord had sent me—I who was separated from my own family—these helpers when I was in distress. It is thanks to dear Arnold and to this family that I am still alive. They took care of me in the most touching way, gave me everything that I needed, since I must always take care not to overexert myself.

But now I have found good people again who are taking good care of me. Yesterday, they cooked me a good semolina pudding, my afternoon coffee, thank God. From a good friend I received a beautiful care package, and Friday I received from dear Else an <u>excellent</u> big cake and various other things. These things were very much <u>appreciated</u>, since my box of supplies was totally empty. You cannot imagine the happiness when a package like that is delivered to you and with what great appetite everything is relished.

Your loving, thankful,

Dora

P.S. I wrote to my dears in Kfar Shmaryahu last week via Tangiers, Morocco. I hope to hear from them directly one day. I'm writing in great haste, the door is open, so I can see better to write.

———

This is the one letter Dora wrote from Gurs that had a bit of hope and "happiness"; this lifting of the spirits was largely due to the thought of being relocated. Indeed, a great change was under way at Gurs. Dora was witnessing a large population transfer. In February, Gurs had approximately 12,250 internees; by April, there were 7,000. More than 1,200 of the elderly were sent to smaller camps at Noé and Récébédou. It is unclear why Dora was not selected; perhaps she was too weak to travel. Families with children up to the age of fifteen, a total of 4,500 individuals, were transferred to the internment camp at Rivesaltes.[42] In each case the internees were being sent to camps where the conditions were notably better.[43]

Dora watched as fellow internees, some of whom had perhaps offered her a bit of their food packages, cared for her when she was ill, or maybe even given her some financial assistance, packed their limited belongings, said their good-byes, and boarded transport vehicles. The transfer, as one aid worker explained, was a severe blow to those left behind at Gurs.

Although Dora had been correct about the exodus, she had been wrong to assume that she was to be part of this transfer to newer camps where conditions were said to be somewhat better. She was not relocated but stayed in the darkness of barrack 9 in Ilot K.

Dora had closed her letter commenting that she needed to write in haste since the door was open. It is a somewhat strange ending for the letter. Why the need for an open door? A report filed by a relief worker clarifies the statement. "When we entered the barrack, I could not see a thing, but only feel and hear a great many people crowded around me." He had entered a structure with no lights or windows, a world of perpetual night. Describing a similar infirmary barrack, the aid worker states,

> When we stepped inside the room seemed totally dark. Later when our eyes were adjusted to the darkness we could see a tiny glimmer of light at the far end of the room ... I remember jumping back in alarm when I stumbled over a strangely detached limb on the floor, and feeling reassured to see that it was only a wooden one. But in that dark barrack where the atmosphere was heavy with suffering and despair one felt that nameless horrors ducked in the shadows.[44]

In February 1941, nearly one hundred barracks at Gurs had been equipped with windows. It was said that "where windows had been installed the internees have gathered new courage to bear their tragic fate."[45] Apparently, windows had not yet been placed in Dora's barrack, and so she could write only when the door was open.

———

To: Arnold Hatch, Albany, New York
From: Dora Hecht, Camp de Guerre, Passes Pyrénées, France
Date: June 6, 1941
Translated from the German

Dear Arnold!

Yet another week has passed without receiving a sign of life from you. It has now been exactly a quarter of a year that I haven't heard anything more from you. I can't explain the reason for your silence. I don't know if you received my letters from March and April (sent by registered mail). I also never received an answer to various inquiries. At the moment I am totally at the end of my resources. The burn wound on my arm that took four months to heal cost me a lot of money, and also the family that took care of me.

And yet I was lucky that I found someone to look after me, that I didn't have to go out in the wind and weather— that would have been impossible. What next winter will bring is something I am not worried about yet. I wrote to you last week about my illness. My heart is just weak. I can't do anything except take digitalis and rest as much as possible. Life in the barracks is certainly not beneficial to my condition, but alone what is left for me? I am just acquiescing to the inevitable.

It is so sad to be here totally alone and now also destitute and sick. I certainly wouldn't have begged you for support of any kind, even linen and articles of clothing, if I didn't need them so urgently. From the amount that I received from you in March, I have handed 75 francs over to the social committee—now one must hand over 5 percent of the amount received. Last Friday I had a severe blackout and fell unconscious to the ground. They laid me on my cot, and when I regained consciousness I heard someone asking, "Is she dead?"

A lady in the barracks where I am staying, <u>Miss Cäcilie Ettinger</u>, is willing to advance me some money for a telegram to you if she receives money from America in the next few days. In case I should no longer be alive by then, could I trouble you to <u>kindly reimburse</u> her cost of the telegram? Under no circumstances can she come for the money, as we all live off of handouts. Yesterday she brought me a cup of hot cocoa, and the day before she brought me oatmeal soup. I thanked her for both with all my heart.

From a French nurse I received a donation of a cup of apple marmalade. And I have now received Quakerspeisung three times for one week—that's all. And you write that you are contributing to relief organizations. How badly do I need a few very simple sports dresses, or material to make some. They don't need to be new—a pinafore could replace a dress in hot weather. I urgently need a <u>wool vest</u> and a coat—I am medium-sized and slim, approximately like Aunt Ida—warm stockings, because here we have here more rain than sun.

How nice it would have been for me if I had been able to accompany my loved ones two years ago.

Dear Arnold, you wrote to me in your last letter on

January 28th that you wished I could be with you. And believe me, I would prefer a thousand times to be with my dearest relatives than alone and abandoned in a foreign country. And now one request: please let me know how you are doing, and why I don't hear from you?

Best wishes to you from all my heart, and thank you for all of the sacrifices you have made on my behalf. Your greetings from October along with 500 Marks were still lying at the German bank in B. B., as well as the last monthly assistance from you at the time of my departure.

With my love to <u>you all,</u>
Your thankful cousin Dora

———

There was little to be done for Dora Hecht, interned in Ilot K of Camp Gurs. However, other family members, such as Alfons, still hoped for a way out of Germany.

13

A Closing Door

To: Luzie Hatch, New York

From: Alfons Isack, Essen, Germany

Date: May 18, 1941

Translated from the German

My dear friends, dear Luzie:

You're probably surprised to hear from me again. I'm doing well, and my lovely bride is doing fine, too, I hope it's the same for you. I received a return receipt from you, my dear Luzie, but I haven't received a letter yet. Every day I am waiting in anticipation.

My dearest Luzie, have you been able to work something out with Arnold for me? If Arnold isn't willing to sponsor both of us, please make sure he'll provide and affidavit (in English) and arrange passage for me.

I'll be married by the time you receive this letter. I have included a photograph of Marianne and me, so you can get to know her.

Dear Luzie, I don't want to forget to wish you a happy birthday. With all of my heart I wish you the very best for you. It's beautiful that you can celebrate your birthday once again with your parents and Rolf. Have you found work for Edwin and Rolf? Aunt Helen has probably already settled down over there. But now, dearest Luzie, I want to mention one more time [letter ends here]

———

———

To: Luzie Hatch, New York
From: Alfons Isack, Essen, Germany
Date: Undated
Translated from the German

Dear Luzie:

Please make sure that Arnold sends two copies of his sponsorship immediately. One copy has to go to us; the other copy has to go to the consulate in Stuttgart. (Stuttgart, Königstrasse 19 a.). If I indeed were to receive this sponsorship, I would know that you, my dearest Luzie, have contributed to my good fortune. As soon as I get there, I will compensate you for your troubles.

Yours,
Alfons

———

A Closing Door

Marianne's note follows.

<hr />

Dear friends:

I'll take the liberty to address you in an informal manner even though we've never met. I'm happy that I will meet all of you in person soon. It is our greatest desire to immigrate as soon as possible.

We're used to work. There's no work that we're afraid of, and I'm sure that we'll find some way to make a living. We won't rely on your sponsorship.

Our dearest Alfons talked a lot about you, and I'm looking forward to meeting you soon. Please receive my regards for now.

Yours,
Marianne

<hr />

To: Alfons Isack, Essen, Germany
From: Luzie Hatch, New York
Date: June 9, 1941
Translated from the German

My dear Alfons,

First of all, I would like to express, also on behalf of my parents and Rolf, our best and warmest wishes to you and your dear fiancée (probably your wife in the meantime), and we hope with you and for you that you will both very soon be able to live the life that you long for.

Hopefully your plans will be realized in the foreseeable future.

In any case, we were very happy that you, dear Alfons, have found such a kind and pretty wife, which is "visibly" confirmed in the nice little picture that you enclosed. This way you can offer each other support and you can face everything together, which is surely a great relief.

Yesterday Rolf turned eighteen years old. He is now an adult; at least that's what he thinks. At the moment he is working in a slipper factory. Father has also found a small position in a factory. We are happy that we can eke out a living. Mother cleans and cooks.

Now to your request for a guarantee, dear Alfons. You cannot imagine how sorry I am that even today I still do not have encouraging news for you. As I have already written to you many times, it is very difficult to persuade Arnold to offer a guarantee. He certainly wouldn't do it for your wife, since he has already flatly refused to do so for Aunt Martha's husband, as you are probably already aware.

He has a mind of his own, and unfortunately, I have no influence over him. I have not seen him in person at all since last October and have only spoken to him on the telephone maybe three times when he was in New York. I have always mentioned you, but unfortunately so far to no avail. It is possible that he may agree to it at a later time . . . And I can only keep recommending that you approach him directly, since I am not getting anywhere.

Please let me know immediately if you or your wife have any relatives or friends here whom I could approach, as I do not want to leave anything untried in my attempts to help you.

With my very best wishes and all my love and kisses

Luzie

———

Although Luzie had little encouraging news for Alfons, she did have something for her aunt Paula that would surely give comfort, a letter from her daughter, Erna, in Palestine. With Germany and Britain at war and Palestine under the British mandate, there was no direct mail between Germany and Palestine. In order for Paula and her children to communicate, they needed an individual in a neutral country to function as a forwarding house, which added weeks to the delivery time.

Along with Erna's letter, Luzie sent a note with the news that she had decided to bring Paula to America on her own, without Arnold's assistance. Having been in the United States for almost three years, working and saving when possible, Luzie was now somewhat comfortable, even a bit confident.

———

To: Paula Steinberg, Dortmund, Germany
From: Luzie Hatch, New York
Date: June 8, 1941
Translated from the German

My dear, good Aunt Paula,

I only wanted to write once I was able to give you good news. And that is the case today.

You will surely be most happy to receive the attached letter from Erna. I also went ahead immediately and answered her right away, in order to avoid another long standstill in the correspondence.

Your congratulations for my birthday also arrived rather punctually. It was so kind of you to think of that, and now I hope for sure that we will celebrate my 30th!!!! together next year.

When I say that I hope we can celebrate the next birthday together, I must also give an explanation for this hope. Of course, that has to do with the affidavit for you. Unfortunately, I cannot appeal at all to our cousin for that, since he has already refused to take care of the papers for Herta's parents (father's sister in Berkach) and doesn't want to do anything for Werner Hecht and family or for Alfons.

He feels that he had done enough, and despite my truly greatest efforts, I have not been able to dissuade him from that opinion.

Of course, I have also spoken to Aunt Emma and Walter and Grete . . . several times on your behalf. They are not averse to giving an affidavit later, although at the moment it is not possible. But so that you see our good intentions and in order to avoid losing more time with all these preparations . . . (you surely have no idea how tedious all this is), I have decided for the time being that I will arrange a guarantee for you.

I have only a small salary and do not have a whole lot in the bank either, and over the past weeks I have been saving diligently so that it will be more, and I am still saving now.

That is one of the reasons I have not brought the guarantee to the post office yet, because the more that I have saved, the bigger the bank statement and the more the affidavit is worth. Besides, I hardly believe that it is possible to travel overseas at the moment, and since the guarantee is void after a few months, there is not much point in sending it in so early, because then it will surely have to be renewed again.

I have already asked you, do you have any other friends and relatives here (even if they are distant relatives) whom I could approach [for the guarantee]? I will gladly try everything to have you at my side.

Of course, then a big problem would be the question of transportation. How that could be arranged is not yet clear to me. But time will tell. In the worst-case scenario I might have to take out "loans."

I believe that is everything that I can tell you. If it is not exactly very rosy, then at least you will feel the certitude that I am concerned about you and that I will do what I can to the best of my ability, and that you can rely on me and count on me. Continue writing to me about everything that moves you . . .

It is with great regret that I learned of the passing of Uncle Max. It really shocked me even though I also do not begrudge him the well-earned rest. He really endured a lot.

Last week Aunt Lina wrote me a letter . . . and also told me the sad news. She also asked me to procure a guarantee for her and Werner. However, Alfons must not know anything about it, I don't even know if I should be telling you this. But I have no secrets from you . . . In any case, I will answer her directly and not mention anything about my letter to you. Of course, I don't know from whence I should obtain a guarantee for both of them, although I know

September 1939–October 1941

—

242

for sure that they both deserve it and would not be a burden to anyone.

I will write them that they should let me know first of all what friends they have here.

There are a whole lot of people from Essen here ... whom I could potentially approach on their behalf. Then I will tell them that I am willing to possibly also arrange a guarantee for them once your thing is sorted out ... I am really very sorry, because Aunt Lina was always very nice to me and really deserves to lead a happier life.

Alfons has already sent me two registered letters as well, and unfortunately I have to tell him that I cannot help him.

That is all for today. We are all doing very well. More on the family in the next letter.

To Uncle Jakob, <u>as always</u>, my most heartfelt greetings.

Continue writing to me about what your prospects are so that nothing is left untried and no opportunity is missed.

That is all for today.

Your

Luzie

———

Through all of her communication with her cousin Arnold, the time Luzie wrote with the greatest force was in the fall of 1941 when discussing the emigration of Herta Stein's parents. What accounts for this change in her approach? To begin with, after three years in New York, Luzie was no longer an insecure and bewildered immigrant. Nor was she concerned that if she angered Arnold, her parents and half-brother would be left in Shanghai to fend on their own. All three had arrived safely in the United States back in October 1940. Finally, there was her relationship with Herta. The two had sailed to America together and had likely had regular contact since then. All these factors helped Luzie take a stronger stand than usual when advocating that Arnold should help Herta's parents find refuge in Cuba.

———

To: Arnold Hatch, Albany, New York
From: Luzie Hatch, New York
Date: October 11, 1941

Dear Arnold:

I was delighted to learn from Herta that you intend to come to Aunt Ida's and that you would like to meet all of us here. I am really looking forward to seeing you . . .

With us everything is all right. Although nobody of us is earning any big salary we manage to get along because all of us are working and are contributing our share. For the past seven months father has been employed in the same factory; Ralph is now working in the stockroom of the organization I am connected with, and my mother takes care of different apartments and in the evenings helps out at parties. We are only too happy to be together and to be able to live as free human beings.

Herta told me of her correspondence with you regarding the immigration of her parents and that you do not approve of the plan to bring them to Cuba. Dear Arnold, I know that you only want the best for all of us, especially so in Herta's case, and that you only refused to help in this matter because you do not think that the plan will work out.

May I, therefore, explain a few things about this. In the first place, this plan has worked and hundreds of people already arrived in Cuba in the last few weeks and more are leaving Germany daily for the same destination. Only this morning Herta received a cable from the Hilfsverein in Germany, urging to arrange for the Cuba immigration of her parents immediately.

Responsible Jewish organizations in USA will confirm that there is nothing illegal about the whole matter ... As soon as the financial arrangements have been made, the Cuban Government will cable their Consulate in Berlin that the visas have been approved and are to [be] granted to the people in question. Thereupon the respective persons get them immediately and can leave Germany. The whole procedure takes only a few weeks.

Now Herta, who is one of the most economical persons I know, has arranged to take care of everything, but she can't put up an amount of $1,300.00 consisting of:
$500.00 Landing Bond per person (2×500) = $1,000.00
  paid to the Cuban Immigration Department
$150.00 Deposit of return passage (2×150.00) = 300.00
  paid to the same authorities

$1,300.00

This money can under no circumstances be used by the persons when in Cuba—it has only to be deposited as a precautionary measure—and it is given to them when they leave Cuba. By this time Herta will have saved more money so that the amount of $1,300.00 will remain untouched.

Maybe Herta did not explain clearly enough that she

only wants this money from you as a loan and that it will definitely be returned to you. In case her parents would not reach Cuba for any reasons whatsoever, the amount will be refunded right away so that there is no risk at all.

Please, dear Arnold, do think the whole matter over again, as we do not know people who would lend this amount. Herta is so worried and desperate and certainly would not bother you if she knew of any other way. Had the American Consulates in Germany not been closed just before her parents were scheduled to receive their visas, the whole transaction would not have been necessary, but as it is, this is the only way to save them. However, it has to be done as quickly as possible because Herta's parents are in danger of being put in camps where so many perish—any delay may be fateful.

I would not recommend any of this business would I not be convinced that it will work. Furthermore, I am sure that should Herta's parents arrive, they would not be a burden. The start is hard for everybody. But as you experienced with Herta, my family and myself, we tried not to bother you once we arrived in this country. The same will be true of Herta's parents. Her father will find a job in a factory or so, and her mother will certainly be able to help in a household. As they are very modest, and Herta will always earn money, too, they will have enough to make their living.

Now, dear Arnold, don't think that I want to talk you into something. I wrote you in such detail in order to give you a clear picture of the situation, and you may ask any organization or traveling bureau in Albany for verification of my statements. Please talk the matter over with Stephen again and please understand that we only want to save two relatives from certain destruction.

I am looking forward with much joy to seeing you on October 28th.

Best regards and kisses,

Yours, as ever,

Luzie

———

———

To: Luzie Hatch, New York

From: Arnold Hatch, Albany, New York

Date: October 20, 1941

Dear Luzie:

I have delayed answering your letter of recent date relative to Herta's parents because first of all I had a strike here last week which has just about driven me crazy and secondly because I was making some investigations into this highly unsatisfactory matter of bringing people from Germany into this country via Cuba.

One of the agencies which I contacted seems to make a specialty of this immigration via Cuba, and I send you herewith for your information a copy of a letter which I recently received from them. The second sheet containing what they claim to be full information about this procedure is self-explanatory, and in my opinion it is about as unsatisfactory a thing as you could possibly ask for.

Aside from the question about whether you get any of your money back or not, and I am by no means convinced that you will get all or most of it back, their plan calls for a total deposit of close to $6,000.00 itemized as follows:

Ordering of Cuban Tourist Visa, $2000

per person	$4,000.00
Bond of $500.00 per person	1,000.00
Guarantee for further transportation expenses	
per person	150.00
Cost of formalities, $235.00 per person	470.00

This whole plan is outrageously expensive, and in spite of what you and Herta and others have told me is not guaranteed nor is the return of the principal investment guaranteed if these people cannot be located in Germany, if they cannot get to port, if they cannot get out of Cuba promptly, or a lot of other ifs.

It is perfectly obvious that the Cuban immigration authorities are working this thing for all it is worth—capitalizing on human misery and charging anything they want for doing a dubious job with plenty of graft for everybody undoubtedly in the picture.

I am sorry that I cannot and will not go for this thing, and while I understand Herta's anxiety about her parents this is a little bit too much for me, and I ask you to tell her that I will not consider it under any circumstances, and I hope that you will accept this as final.

I was glad to note from your letter that you are well, happy, and comfortable, and I am going to make every effort to be down in New York on the 28th and expect to see you all then.

Yours, as ever,

Arnold

—

September 1939–October 1941

—

To: Arnold Hatch, Albany, New York
From: Luzie Hatch, New York
Date: October 23, 1941

Dear Arnold:

I thank you very much for your kind letter of Oct. 20th. After studying it carefully, I venture to write you again as I have a feeling that there seems to be some kind of misunderstanding. You evidently are under the impression that if you give $1,300.00 you may also be asked to put up much more and perhaps as much as $6,000.00.

Please let me explain that Herta can arrange for the two required Letters of Credits of $2,000.00 each by financing this against payment of $150.00 each. She will instruct her parents upon their arrival in Cuba not to draw from these Letters of Credit under any circumstances and will take care of their living expenses in Cuba from the money she will have saved again by this time and her daily earnings. (By the way, this amount of $2,000.00 per person is not for "ordering of Cuban Tourist Visas"). Furthermore, Herta will take care of $235.00 per person for formalities which include ordering of Cuban visas.

Herta is quite aware of the fact that these two amounts (2 × $150.00 = $300.00 and 2 × $235.00 = $470.00) may not be refunded in case her parents should not reach Cuba for any reason whatsoever. However, she made up her mind to sacrifice all she worked for in three years in order to try everything to save her parents—she would not have a quiet minute for the rest of her life would she not take every possible step for her parents whom she loves so much.

Now you see that the money she wants you to lend for a couple of months is needed after everything else has already been taken care of, and for the sole purpose of putting up the required bonds, namely the amount of $1,300.00. This money is absolutely refundable which fact will be confirmed to you by a letter you will receive from the Compass Resettlement Service Inc. They did not make this clear in their information to you of Oct. 17th. Since I am under the impression that you made your decision having a sum of $6,000.00 in mind, I take the liberty of asking you again for help, that means for a loan of $1,300.00.

Please dear Arnold, wouldn't you reconsider the matter in this light. As something has to be done right away in order to save Herta's parents from being shipped to Poland or elsewhere, will you please be kind enough to call Herta up after receipt of this letter. The most important thing is to get the matter started so that Herta can cable her parents and the Hilfsverein that the Cuba immigration will be arranged. This will be a protection for them; as it would prove to the authorities that they will be leaving Germany anyhow.

Should the sum of $1,300.00 not be convenient to you, would you then be willing to help with part of this amount? In this case we would have to ask everybody we know for some money as a loan in order to get the amount together. You can imagine how difficult this would be, but it would have to be done.

The main thing, dear Arnold, is, whatever your decision may be, that you please call Herta upon receipt of this letter, because there is no minute to be lost at this time and proceedings have to be started without delay.

September 1939–October 1941

—

I want to apologize for being so insistent but you will certainly understand that this is a question of life or destruction for two relatives.

I do hope that you will be able to come to New York on the 28th—and as far as I am concerned I shall try my very best to make it a pleasant meeting and to keep unpleasant matters away from you.

With much love, I am

Yours, as ever,

Luzie

———

As for another of Luzie's frequent correspondents, Dora Hecht, news came from an unlikely source. In early November 1941, Arnold received a letter from Havana, Cuba, sent by an unknown Max Hirschkind. To Arnold's surprise, he turned out to be yet another one of his German relatives. But Max was not writing for assistance, a fact that must have relieved Arnold, but rather to inform Arnold that Aunt Dora had died. In addition to his note for Arnold, Max Hirschkind enclosed a letter for his aunt Marta, uncle Leo, and cousin Rudolph. Not having their Palestine address, he hoped that Arnold would forward them his note, which explained much.

———

To: Rosenfeld Family, Palestine
From: Max Hirschkind, on board the SS *Marques de Camillas*
Date: October 13, 1941
Translated from the German

Dear Aunt Martha, dear Uncle Leo and dear Rudi,
A time rich in sorrow and distress, seemingly intermi-

nable, is our lot. For the longest time you have heard nothing from me, from my family, from any of us. Now I will report to you in broad strokes:

On 07/06/40 I drove with wife and child from Wiesbaden to Brussels. On 05/10/40, Belgium was pulled into the war. I was interned, and France was "done in." The dreadful camps of St.-Cyprien and Gurs are now behind me. Now my dear wife and our little boy are traveling with me to Cuba. Both of my loved ones followed me to France of their own accord. Through artillery fire they made their way to find husband and father.

In June/July 1940 they themselves were interned at Gurs for seven weeks. Then they came to St. Cyprien-Plage, and until the end of October 1940 we saw each other nearly every day for a few hours, albeit under punishing conditions.

Then we were separated again for five months. I came to Gurs. I heard that the approximately 8,000 people, young and old, who were housed in the various surrounding units, were Jewish people from Baden and the Palatinate. The good Aunt Dora, who in the meantime had heard that "people from Belgium" had arrived, searched for us, as I did for her.

We found each other promptly, and our delight at seeing each other was extraordinary and emotional. We all had a grim lot, and Aunt Dora certainly did not count among the old people. She was surrounded by good people (in the Women's Barracks 9 of Women's Lot K). Every fourteen days I visited our good aunt. Oftentimes I was not allowed to, i.e., I had to give up the very scarce exit passes to fellow internees who needed to visit their wives and mothers.

Aunt Dora bore her lot with courage and heroism. Shared suffering is a lighter burden to bear. Surely I don't need to mention that I also brought along and smuggled in whatever I could for the good Aunt Dora. I immediately asked her about her resources and heard that Mr. Arnold Hatch was providing for her brilliantly. When his bank transfers didn't arrive on time, I was happy to provide her with the essentials. She would reimburse me later.

My efforts to transfer the good Aunt Dora to a better camp failed, partly of her own volition, as she did not want to leave her surroundings. (On the whole, I couldn't do much, but still, I had established relationships.)

On February 28th I was able to leave Gurs. Sick leave. It was not a cover, I was indeed sick. On 02/27/41, I bade farewell to our dear aunt, and after that we corresponded. For a long time my last postcard went unanswered. I wrote again . . . Again I waited. Now it is with a heavy heart that I must inform you that a letter arrived from Prof. Adler (Hôpital Central) with the terribly sad news:

Dear Mr. Hirschkind,

I am writing to inform you of the sad news of Mrs. Dora Hecht's passing. She passed away in the Infirmerie Centrale of the Gurs Camp, today, September 3rd at 1:30 pm. Prior to her demise, the deceased asked me to send this news to you.

Please allow me to express my condolences on this painful occasion.

Signed Abraham Adler

And now, my dears please believe me that I share your

sorrow and that, with great emotion. I take your hand in condolence. Surely I need only to mention briefly that in my conversations with the dearly departed very often the subject was her love and loyalty to you.

Immediately thereafter I made further inquiries with the head of the division who, through a friend who knows her well, answered me:

Cause of death: heart condition, eight-day-long illness.

Buried 09/05 in the presence of Rabb. Altmann, Karlsruhe.

Further it reads: a headstone can be placed. Cost: fr. 300/350–, to be sent to the rabbinate G/i.

Jewelry: consists of one watch, turned in to the Commandant's Office.

Money: nothing was available, on the contrary. Miss Cäcilie Ettinger from Barrack 9 (her neighbor in the adjacent bed) had lent her fr. 150– in cash.

A thoroughly damaged suitcase is still on hand and remains here in the barracks. Stationery that was found in her handbag was handed in directly to the Commandant's Office. No dresses were available but rather only a few blouses, which were bequeathed to occupants of the barracks who had been helpful and supportive to her.

Among her papers she had a will, according to which she bequeathed everything to Miss Cäcilie Ettinger, Barrack 9. But all of these papers were handed in to the Commandant's Office. The address of the cousin is: Mr. A. Hatch—

This last correspondence came into my hands on 10/03/41. Before that, we were in Marseille for fourteen days to make arrangements for our migration to Cuba. I have now instructed my friend and comrade Kurt Simons, Meillon B.P., to receive further communications and to arrange:

1) For fr. 150– to be sent to Miss Ettinger
2) That a (makeshift) headstone be placed for fr. 350–

Now I come to our loved ones: my dearest little mother; I did not inform her of Aunt Dora's passing. Aunt Lilli and Uncle Theobald are still in Wiesbaden. My in-laws (in Bussum—Holland) write that they are well. Beate is in England and has found a secretarial job.

Woe is me when I think of the separation and the sorrow, the misery and the hardships of these dear ones—but may we persevere!

Now I will end with my best wishes for your health, and sending you my most heartfelt and loyal greetings.

Your Max

———

Arnold wasted no time in responding to Max's request. The very day after he had received the note, he forwarded it to Palestine. Knowing that Rudolph and his parents had loved Dora dearly, Arnold did his best to offer some comfort, although he acknowledged that his words might sound callous. "I can only extend to you all my heartfelt sympathy in this great and unnecessary tragedy, and would suggest that you try to get yourself in the frame of mind where you see that this unfortunate lady is better off."

In the early morning of December 7, 1941, 353 Japanese fighters, bombers, and torpedo planes attacked Pearl Harbor. The surprise and force of the assault resulted in a devastating death toll:

A Closing Door
—

2,404 men were killed and 1,282 wounded. The next day the United States declared war on Japan. A declaration of war on Germany and Italy followed on December 11. War had come to the United States.

There would be no more letters or cables to Aunt Martha, Aunt Paula, or Cousin Alfons and his new wife, Marianne. Now those in the West and in Palestine would wait and wonder about the conditions of their German relatives, likely altering between periods of hope and piercing fear.

During this time the one person Luzie corresponded with regularly was her close friend from L. S. Mayer, Hans Hirschfield, who had found refuge in Canada. On August 15, 1945, the day of Japan's surrender, Luzie could write Hans the best letter of all.[1]

VICTORY-DAY!!!!
August 15, 1945

Dear Hans:

What a day!! What a pleasure to sit down to write to a soldier friend in the knowledge that he is probably even happier than we civilians are. At last we have peace again—I hope the people all over the world have learned their terrible lesson well, and will know how to get along with each other. My best wishes for a speedy release—what are your chances in this direction?

Congratulations on becoming a Canadian citizen; that was really a nice birthday present. We shall drink to that on your next visit to New York which I hope will take place soon.

September 1939–October 1941

I just returned from my vacation, which I spent in Connecticut. I had a very relaxing time—just what I wanted and needed. It seems that I am too intense for this world, or for the people in it, or for those I get involved with—and I've decided to take things less seriously and am now very anxious for the results of this drastic decision.

My brother was transferred to the Philippines, where he arrived a few weeks ago. He is very happy about this change, after having spent a year and a half in New Guinea. Those guys in the Pacific surely must be relieved.

How is your business? And how is your girl friend?

I am still with the American Jewish Committee—the longest job I ever had. We'll see what the future brings. I wonder whether L.S.M. will do business all over the world again—I wouldn't be surprised, they are very enterprising people.

In case I shouldn't write you soon again, I want to take this opportunity to send you my very best wishes for the New Year, a New Year which I hope will find you a civilian again settled down to a normal and enjoyable life.

As ever,

Luzie

———

CONCLUSION

"I am wondering if you could get any information for me with reference to the whereabouts of Alfons Isack, Martha Marchand, and Norbert Hecht." The instructions, written two weeks after the German surrender in May 1945, came from Arnold's younger brother, Stephen Hatch.

Arnold had died of a heart attack on October 20, 1943, the very day the strike at his plant had been settled. Perhaps the stress of the labor dispute aggravated his medical condition and contributed to his early death at the age of fifty-five. Having cared so long for many of his relatives, he himself did not live to see the end of the war. Stephen had taken over both the business and the family responsibilities. "I presume," Stephen added in his note to Luzie, "that these people are all in Germany, and I am desirous of ascertaining if they survived the war."

Alfons Isack, who had been the most persistent in his efforts to leave, was first imprisoned in his town of Essen and later deported to the Theresienstadt Ghetto in Czechoslovakia on July 21, 1942. He managed to survive in the ghetto for slightly over two years and was once again deported, this time to Auschwitz-Birkenau, on September 29, 1944. He was, according to Yad Vashem records, murdered at Auschwitz.

Martha Marchand had pleaded for assistance in taking the Trans-Siberian route out of Germany. In trying to advance Martha's case, Luzie argued to Arnold that many had taken the route and survived.

In fact, some did successfully manage the Trans-Siberian route, but their number was not great. Moise Moiseff, vice president of the Jewish community of Kobe, Japan, in his report "Jewish Transits in Japan," recorded that from July 1940 to May 1941, a total of 4,664 refugees had entered Japan, of which 2,498 were German Jewish refugees.[1] With the Nazi invasion of Russia in June 1941, this exit route, which had brought a few thousand refugees to safety, was closed.

Martha and her family were never able to leave Germany. Martha, her daughter, Ruth, and her husband, Alfred, were transported to the Lodz Ghetto in Poland, which is listed as their place of death in the Yad Vashem Archives.[2]

Luzie's Aunt Paula Steinberg also remained trapped in Germany, unable to fulfill her wish of joining her children in Palestine. Her daughter, Erna Mendels, submitted a page of testimony to the

Yad Vashem Archives citing Paula's date of death as April 27, 1942. No place of death was provided.

When Luzie and her younger cousin Herta Stein had set sail for America in the immediate aftermath of Kristallnacht, each left behind her parents, promising to assist them once settled in the United States. In actuality, as the one with more age, life experience, and access to Arnold, it was Luzie who largely shouldered the burden of attempting to bring Herta's parents, Salomon and Elsa Stein, out of Nazi Germany. Their plan had been to go to Cuba, and Luzie had forcefully pleaded their case to Arnold, hoping that he would grant financial assistance. Yet the couple never made it to this Caribbean Island nor to any other refuge. They are listed on the October 5, 1942, deportation from Thuringia, Germany. Although no specific camp is cited, it is believed that they both perished.

An estimated 160,000–200,000 German Jews perished in the Holocaust. Alfons Isack, Paula Steinberg, Martha Marchand Harf and her family, Salomon and Elsa Stein, and Dora Hecht, who died in Vichy France, were part of this horrific statistic. Repeatedly, they had asked Luzie for help. Her failure to rescue them remained with Luzie for the rest of her life. There were probably times, many times, when she tried to subdue this dragon of guilt with logic and reason. What power did she really have to alter their circumstances? After all, she was a young, single woman existing on a modest income, adjusting to a new life in the United States, while worrying about her family members caught in the Nazi vise. And Luzie, like thousands of other Americans attempting to rescue relatives abroad, found herself struggling with a range of complicated and unwelcoming immigration laws. Were these not compelling reasons for her failure? Yet, when logic and emotion duel, the latter can be an indomitable force.

Conclusion
—

Of course, Luzie included her great success in bringing her stepmother, father, and half-brother, Rolf, to the United States. Her father, having arrived in New York at middle age, would never again work as a department store executive. He became a factory worker, and his wife, Helene, had to work as a housekeeper. In 1943, Luzie's young brother, now named Ralph, received what he called "a message from the President of the United States," or "greetings from the draft." He entered the army in February 1943 and after training was sent to the Philippines. Like thousands of GIs, Ralph benefited from the GI Bill and pursued a college education after returning home. He became a social studies teacher and taught history and geography from 1949 to 1984.

Luzie's friend and business associate Stefan Pauson would eventually once again be involved in the basket trade. He and his wife would remain in England for the remainder of their lives. His son, Peter, who due to his small frame and spectacled face had been teased and called "professor" by his German classmates, did, in fact, go on to become a professor, teaching organic chemistry at Strathclyde University in Scotland and garnering international recognition for his research work. Pauson's daughters, Eva and Hella, would find their way to the United States, where they would marry, work, and raise their families.

The Friedländer family, the Hechts' Berlin neighbors, would also make their way to the United States, but not before enduring a tragedy. The young man whom Inge had married in 1940 died two years later after he contracted typhoid. She would eventually remarry and leave for the United States in 1946 with her second husband and infant son, settling in New York City and reuniting with her parents, who had arrived there a few months earlier.

Hans Hirschfield, Luzie's close friend from L. S. Mayer, had arrived in Canada neither through design nor desire but through the winds of good fortune. Hans soon found it to be an environment that suited him well. He would remain in Canada, marrying a Canadian Jewish woman and raising three children. His prior experience at L. S. Mayer was put to good use. For more than thirty years he ran his firm, the Horizon Company of Canada, importing giftware, housewares, and stationery. Business matters would take him to various parts of the world, including his native city of Berlin.

Although many immigrants such as Luzie and Hans's brothers changed and anglicized their names, Hans refused to do so. He would always remain Hans Egon Hirschfeld, firmly declaring, "I lived my life as myself." Hans Hirschfeld died in the late 1990s.

In Luzie's early years in New York, she had always thought that, like Hans, she would eventually return to merchandising, a world she loved. However, when Luzie entered the American Jewish Committee in 1938, she had found her professional home. Her entire career, from 1938 to 1977, with the exception of two brief interludes, was at AJC.

It was her German heritage that had first helped Luzie to secure her position. A native German was needed to assist in reading, translating, and organizing the incoming German newspapers, articles, and documents that would be used to write the *White Book*. After the war, her German background continued to be of use. Within the institutional world of American Jewry, it was Luzie's employer, the American Jewish Committee, that was at the forefront of building a roadway to reconciliation with Germany.

In 1960, a group of visiting German educators who had traveled to four American cities to observe American methods of teaching social and civic education, concluded their trip with a daylong conference at the American Jewish Committee. Throughout the 1960s, AJC would remain involved with these educator missions. It is highly likely that Luzie, due to her background, had some involvement with these conferences.

Ironically, her major work on reconciliation would be four years after her retirement when, in 1981, AJC and the Konrad Adenauer Foundation of Germany launched an exchange program that exists to this day. German participants take part in a ten-day course on the American Jewish community while their American counterparts have a similarly intensive look at Germany.

It was natural that Luzie assist in this work. In addition to her fluency in German was her ease and comfort in being with Germans. Gerri Rozanski, the AJC staffer responsible for organizing the missions recalls, "Remember this was the eighties, not many in the Jewish community were so willing to meet with Germans. At the time it was a challenge for us to fill missions to Germany. We were not so far removed for the war. The nature of the loss was much more direct."[3]

And so it was Luzie Hatch who greeted the incoming German delegations and traveled with them not only in New York but to their visits to other parts of America. "Luzie helped make them feel more comfortable in the U.S. She was everyone's familiar grandmother," notes Rozanski. Just as important, she explains, although their parents were reluctant to speak about Nazi Germany, Luzie was willing. "Luzie enabled them to have a conversation about prewar Germany that they couldn't have with their family back home."[4]

There was another reason why the young visiting Germans took to Luzie: she accepted them. Her anger was with the Nazis, not the German people as a whole. Yet this very element of her personality that obviously appealed to visiting German delegations was problematic for some of her Jewish colleagues, who believed she exaggerated the distinction between the Nazis and the German people in terms of both degree and numbers. She was, in their opinion, too quick to forgive.

How she came to this state of reconciliation is unknown. Did it take years, and were there certain events that pushed her in this direction? The documents she left behind offer no answers. But to those who knew her in her later years, it was clear that she retained a love of her native land. A neighbor from her apartment building spoke of Luzie as a German Jew who was very conscious of being German. Her colleague Gerri Rozanski recalls that Luzie once revealed, "I had a beautiful life in Germany. I love the life I had and I miss it. I refuse to think ill of the life I had because of what happened." Her coworker wondered if perhaps there was an element of denial in Luzie's thinking. "That is a question we will never have the answer to," she states. "But I never judged her. I didn't walk in those shoes. I adored her."[5]

Those who met Luzie through the Konrad Adenauer Exchange also adored Luzie. After returning to Germany, many exchange participants maintained their relationship with Luzie through correspondence. Although she was a volunteer rather than a paid staffer, Luzie Hatch became the "face" of AJC's involvement for those at the Konrad Adenauer Foundation in Berlin.

In 1992, the Federal Republic of Germany recognized Luzie's work on building bridges between American Jews and Germans. She was awarded its Order of Merit. In a letter to Luzie, Chancellor Helmut Kohl of Germany wrote:

For many years now, the American Jewish Committee, in cooperation with political foundations in Germany, has or-

Conclusion
—

ganized exchange programs and meetings between young people on this and the other side of the Atlantic. The many young Germans who were privileged to meet you through these programs became attached to you. Thus, a large number of friends will be with you in spirit as you are presented with The Cross of the Order of Merit.[6]

When Luzie received this honor on September 24, 1992, at the German consulate in New York, she noted in her response:

Today, almost 60 years after the Holocaust and the events leading up to it, what happened is history. Nevertheless, I feel that no meaningful shape can be given to the future without acquainting the younger generations with the past. They are burdened with the past, but one cannot hold young people responsible for the sins of their parents and grandparents.

There are some in my generation who feel that I am wasting my time—but I believe that if there was any reason for my own survival, it was to help bring about some kind of reconciliation . . . This kind of reconciliation cannot be achieved through evasion or denials; the past cannot and must not be forgotten. Only if we acknowledge and confront it honestly will we be able to build that bridge between past and future.[7]

In 1943, five years after Luzie arrived in New York City, she had written to her friend Hans Hirschfeld informing him that she was applying for her citizenship papers. "I know how much I owe this wonderful country and I am really thankful for the chance of living here—and I hope to become a good American citizen soon." In September 2001, Luzie Hatch died. She had been a good citizen.

Conclusion
—

I visited Luzie's studio apartment on a number of occasions, each time hoping that within her file cabinets and desk drawers I might find documents that could provide context to the letters. On my final visit, as I closed the door and glanced at the packed bookshelves and the table right next to her bed with a small TV from the 1970s, I thought, "My God, a lifetime was spent right here in this small space."

Did the sales clerks at the nearby bakery or newspaper store wonder, "What happened to that gregarious old woman with the German accent? She hasn't been here in a while." But I knew that thought, if it had occurred at all, would have been fleeting. As I walked to the train station, I could not help but think that although she had walked these streets for decades, the memory of Luzie Hatch would in a short time fade away.

These were the thoughts I had before I delved into the correspondence. In truth, her life was never in any way confined to her apartment or neighborhood. During the war years she had been a hub, sending and receiving messages from distant locations: Bolivia, England, France, Germany, Shanghai, and Canada. And following the war, her work at AJC reconnected with her former homeland. Her living space had been small; her reach had never been limited.

In researching this book, many of Luzie's old connections were, in some way, revived. To the best of my ability, I reconstructed her old network of family and friends—not with the original correspondents, most of whom have died, but with their descendants. Time and again, individuals were stunned to answer the phone and learn that the person on the other end was holding World War II correspondence from their parent, grandparent, or cousin. And as they gave me information, I also offered them new material and details

Conclusion
—

of their family history. Once again, Luzie was a focal point connecting people wide and far.

I had thought that Luzie would simply melt into the abyss of lost memory, but with the publication of *Exit Berlin*, I realize that this is not to be.

APPENDIX

Documents No. 1 and 2 are from the Trials of War Criminals before the Nuernberg Military Tribunals Under Control Council Law No. 10, *vol. 13 (Washington, DC: US Government Printing Office, 1952).*

No. 1. Correspondence from the Files of the Foreign Office, 29 and 31 October 1940, Concerning the Deportation of Jews from Baden and the Palatinate to Unoccupied France

Memorandum from Heydrich's office to the Foreign Office, 29 October 1940

[Handwritten] Enclosure 2
Berlin SW 11, 29 October 1940
Prinz-Albrecht-Strasse 8
Telephone No. 12 00 40

The Chief of the Security Police and of the SD
IV D 4 2602 /40
When replying please quote above file number

[Handwritten] Z D III 4761

To the Foreign Office attention SA Standartenfuehrer Minister Luther Berlin

The Fuehrer ordered the deportation of the Baden Jews via Alsace, and of the Palatinate [Pfalz]¹ Jews via Lorraine. The operation having been carried out to conclusion, I can now report to you that the railway transports left from Baden on 22 and 23 October 1940, and 2 railway transports left the Palatinate on 22 October 1940, with *6,504 Jews*, by prearranged agreement with the local officers of the Wehrmacht, without previous notification of the French authorities. They were transferred into unoccupied France via Chalon-sur-Saône.

The deportation of the Jews took place in all localities of Baden and the Palatinate without friction and without incidents.

The operation itself was scarcely realized by the population.

The registration of the Jewish property values, as well as their trustee administration and utilization will follow through the competent Regierungspraesidenten [heads of regional administration].

Jews living in a mixed marriage were exempted from the transports.
[Illegible signature]

No. 2. Memorandum from Luther of Department Germany, 31 October 1940

[Handwritten]
Filed on 25 Nov
To be resubmitted on 11 Feb [Stamp] SECRET
[Handwritten] to D III 157 secret
Memorandum

Subject: Evacuation of Jews from the Districts Saar-Palatinate and Baden.

On 22 and 23 October 1940, upon order by the Fuehrer, all Jews from the districts of the Saar-Palatinate and Baden have been deported to unoccupied France in nine special trains. The State Police Regional offices in Karlsruhe, Neustadt a.d.H. and Saarbruecken had the order from the Reich Leader SS to prepare and carry out this action in secret. In the morning of 22 October at 0600 hours the Jews were awakened; they had the possibility of getting food supplies and of taking with them 50kg. of luggage. In 9 special trains, of which 7 came from the district of Baden and 2 from the Saar-Palatinate, the Jews were deported via Alsace, resp. Lorraine. A total of 6,504 Jews were comprised in this action. The action went off smoothly and almost unnoticed by the public.

[Handwritten] I/V.A.A. Wako in the Embassy in Paris have instruction to treat the matter in a dilatory manner.

[Initial] R

6 December

[Handwritten] [Initial] R

As SS Hauptsturmbannfuehrer Guenter of the Reich Security Main Office told me, it was contemplated to inform the French Government. But this was refrained from for unknown reasons. All the trains went via Chalon s/Saône. The Armistice Commission has requested instruction as to how to behave toward the French who have demanded a clarification.

Herewith submitted to Minister Luther

[Signed] Luther

Berlin, 31 October 1940

Referat D III

[Handwritten] Klingenhoefer

[Handwritten]
To Bureau RAM, with request to ask for instruction by the Reich Foreign Minister regarding the last paragraph.

[Signed] Luther 31 October

[Initials] LI 2 November

Immediately

Document No. 3 is from the Politischen Archiv, Berlin, Id #AA, R, 100869.

No. 3. Report on the Deportation of German Jews to Southern France, Karlsruhe in Baden-Württemberg, October 30, 1940

By the order of the Gauleiter and Reichsstatthalter Josef Bürckel, residing temporarily in Metz, and Gauleiter Wagner, residing temporarily in Strassburg, the following actions were taken: During the night of October 22, 1940, the Gestapo, with the help of auxiliary police, put all Jews from Baden and Saarpfalz under house arrest. They were deported shortly thereafter by train. In Saarpfalz, the police issued a deportation order to all people involved. The order had been issued on October 20, 1940, by the Gauleiter and Reichsstatthalter in Metz.

Due to an agreement that was made by the armistice commission in Wiesbaden between General von Stülpnagel (Germany) and General Huntzinger (France) and the Vichy Government, the following steps were taken: All <u>French</u> Jews from Alsace-Lorraine are to be deported into unoccupied France; the French authorities are obliged to accommodate the deportees.

The same agreement was used by the involved Gauleiters, who are responsible for Baden and Saarpfalz, to deport <u>all German Jews</u> who reside in Baden and Saarpfalz. Ca. 6300 German Jews were deported from Baden to Southern France; ca. 1150 from Saarpfalz were deported.

The Vichy Government objected to our plans to deport all Jews from the Old Reich, Austria, and the Protectorate of Bohemia and Moravia, ca. 270.000 mostly older people, to France. For this reason, we have delayed the deportation of Jews from Hesse for now.

+++

The deportation of Jews from Baden and Saarpfalz was executed according to the order of the Gauleiter "that all members of the Jewish race have to be deported <u>as long as they can travel</u>." Age or sex was not taken into consideration. We made some exceptions when it came to mixed marriages. Even men who had been <u>fighting for Germany</u> in World War I and their officers, had to be deported. The old age homes in Mannheim, Karlsruhe, Ludwigshafen and so forth were emptied out. Men and women who were unable to walk were put on stretchers and put on trains. The oldest deportee was a 97-year-old man from Karlsruhe. The deportees were given between 15 and 90 minutes to get ready. A number of women and men used this time to avoid deportation by committing suicide. Until Tuesday morning, we counted 8 <u>suicides</u> in Mannheim and 3 <u>suicides</u> in Karlsruhe. We used army vehicles to transport people to the collection points. According to the order, the deportees had to leave behind all of their belongings, financial assets and real estate holdings. We are waiting for a final decision by the Gauleiter, but for now these valuables are being overseen by a trustee. Since in many cases the expatriation was done unlawfully, meaning that a fee for leaving the Reich was not properly paid, we have frozen all assets. We granted each deportee between 10 and 100 Reichsmark; they were mostly exchanged for French francs. We permitted luggage up to 50 pounds. The apartments and houses were sealed by the police.

+++

As far as we know, it took a few days for the 12 sealed-off trains to reach the concentration camps at the foot of the Pyrenees. There won't be enough appropriate housing or food for the often older deportees, and as far as we know the French government contemplates sending them to Madagascar as soon as the ocean route opens up.

NOTES

How It All Began

1. Rafael Medoff, *FDR and the Holocaust: A Breach of Faith* (Washington, DC: David S. Wyman Institute for Holocaust Studies, 2013), 2.

2. Ibid.

1. Berlin Beginnings

1. After immigrating to the United States, Rolf Hecht anglicized his first name, changing it to Ralph. Thus, within the letters, he is usually referred to as "Rolf," while in the narrative he is referred to as "Ralph." Although he was Luzie's half-brother, she always spoke of him as her brother.

2. ORT was a Jewish institution that provided agricultural and vocational instruction.

3. Henry Rodwell, phone interview, London, May 2008.

4. Ralph Hatch, personal interview, Monroe Township, NJ, June 2008.

5. Ibid.

6. Saul Friedländer, *Nazi Germany and the Jews*, Vol. 1: *The Years of Persecution, 1933–1939* (New York: Harper Perennial, 1997), 15.

7. John Toland, *Adolf Hitler* (New York: Ballantine Books, 1977), 401.

2. From Hecht to Hatch

1. According to the log of the *Westphalia*, Nathan's sister Ida had not come to the United States with him in 1873.

4. Persistence Rewarded

1. "Seventy-Five Thousand German Jews Get Passover Relief, Record Total," Jewish Telegraphic Agency, April 6, 1936, vol. 1, no. 202.

2. Ibid.

5. Settling In

1. "Twenty-Five Thousand Jews Under Arrest in Wake of Worst Pogrom in Modern German History," Jewish Telegraphic Agency, November 13, 1938, vol. 4, no. 185.

2. Inge Diamond, phone interview, Boca Raton, FL, December 2011.

3. Ibid.

4. Eva Emmerich, personal interview, Pittsburgh, PA, December 2011.

5. Ibid.

6. Ibid.

7. Ibid.

8. Ibid.

6. Looking Back Home

1. Saul Friedländer, *Nazi Germany and the Jews*, Vol. 1: *The Years of Persecution, 1933–1939* (New York: Harper Perennial, 1997), 259.

2. *100 Jahre L. S. Mayer* (1922), Hessisches Wirtschaftsarchiv, Darmstadt.

3. L. S. Mayer's auditor report, 1930, Landesarchiv Berlin.

4. After a design was patented, L. S. Mayer usually entered into monopoly contracts with factories, granting them the exclusive right to produce the item. This was a good strategy: the factories were pleased because monopoly contracts were generally more profitable, and retail clients were pleased because they were assured a supply of unique goods.

5. Marion A. Kaplan, *Between Dignity and Despair: Jewish Life in Nazi Germany* (Oxford: Oxford University Press, 1998), 24.

6. Only the first volume of the *White Book* was published. Eighty thousand copies of *The Jews in Nazi Germany: The Factual Record of Their Persecution by the National Socialists* were printed in 1933. A special effort was made to distribute the book to non-Jews, particularly professionals in the field of journalism. In 1935, ten thousand copies of an enlarged edition were printed.

7. *White Book,* no. 3, chapters 8–11 (New York: American Jewish Committee, 1939), 177.

8. Ibid., 178.

9. Chamber of Industry and Commerce Records for Frankfurt, L. S. Mayer card files, Trade and Industry Archive of Hessen, Darmstadt.

10. Ibid.

11. Strauss's failure to return was also noted by Nazi officials. The Frankfurt Chamber of Commerce entry for L. S. Mayer in November 1938 notes: "The former managing director, the Jew A. Strauss, is currently residing in Italy. Due to recent events in Germany [Kristallnacht] we do not expect him to return."

12. "Pf" is most likely a reference to L. S. Mayer's Pforzheim office.

7. Escape to Shanghai

1. "Billion Mark Fine, Ban on Business Received with Apathy by Reich Jews Faced with Famine," Jewish Telegraphic Agency, November 14, 1938, vol. 4, no. 186.

2. Like most German Jewish students, Ralph Hecht was enrolled in public school when Hitler assumed power in January 1933. However, the 1933 Law Against the Overcrowding of German Schools, which established a quota limiting Jewish registration, ended Ralph's public school studies. Although he would have qualified for an exemption because his father had served in the German army during World War I, his parents decided to remove him from public school and enrolled him in the Theodor Herzl School, a Jewish institution.

3. Steven E. Aschheim, *Brothers and Strangers: The East European Jew in German and German Jewish Consciousness, 1800–1923* (Madison: University of Wisconsin Press, 1982).

4. Ralph Hatch, personal interview, Monroe Township, NJ, June 2008.

5. NDR radio interview, Bonn, August 8, 1991, Hatch Collection, American Jewish Committee Archives.

6. Ibid.

7. G. E. Miller [Mauricio Fresco], *Shanghai: The Paradise of Adventurers* (New York: Orsay, 1937), 401.

8. *Shanghai Ghetto,* dir. Amir Mann and Dana Janklowicz-Mann. Rebel Child Productions, 2002. Film.

9. Ernest G. Heppner, *Shanghai Refuge: A Memoir of the World War II Jewish Ghetto* (Lincoln: University of Nebraska Press, 1993), 52.

10. Ernest O. Hauser, *Shanghai: City for Sale* (New York: Harcourt, Brace, 1940), 240.

11. David Kranzler, *Japanese, Nazis, and Jews* (New York: Yeshiva University Press, 1976), 43.

12. Ibid., 116.

13. Ibid., 85.

14. Heppner, *Shanghai Refuge*, 52.

15. In *Japanese, Nazis, and Jews*, David Kranzler states that the American Jewish Joint Distribution Committee was the most essential of the relief organizations. He contends that it is doubtful that the refugees would have survived without the Joint's assistance.

8. A Widening Circle

1. The *Clipper* was a method of air transport. The carrier depending on the season either stopped in Lisbon or Bermuda before proceeding to Europe. When World War II began, British censors examined the mail of carriers refueling in Bermuda, thereby delaying mail delivery.

2. Alfons Isack Gestapo file, Landesarchiv Nordrhein-Westfalen, Düsselfdorf.

3. Ibid.

4. Silbermann was an L. S. Mayer executive who had managed to leave Germany.

9. Desperate Appeals

1. Hans was likely referring to all the greetings to Luzie from her former L. S. Mayer colleagues that had been added to the end of Muhme's letter of May 5, 1939.

2. Inge Diamond, phone interview, Boca Raton, FL, December 2011.

3. Ibid.

4. Ibid.

5. Both the Hilfsverein Deutschsprechender Juden of Buenos Aires and the HICEM claimed credit for rescuing these refugees. It is likely that each organization assumed a different role. Although the Hilfsverein paid the

disembarkation and travel fees, it appears that the HICEM was responsible for successfully negotiating with the Chilean government and ultimately acquiring Chilean visas for the refugees.

6. Letter from the Hilfsverein Deutschsprechender Juden to Joseph C. Hyman, executive director of the American Jewish Joint Distribution Committee, March 15, 1939, AJDC Archives, Collection 33/44, folder 1069, no. 1 of 2.

7. Ibid.

8. Friedrich Borchardt, Report on Bolivia, May 1939, AJDC Archives, Collection 33/44, folder 1075, no. 1 of 2.

9. Diamond interview.

10. Letter from Sociedad de Protección de los Immigrantes Israelitas, La Paz, Bolivia, to AJDC, Paris, January 16, 1940, AJDC Archives, Collection 33/44, folder 1075.

11. Marion A. Kaplan, *Between Dignity and Despair: Jewish Life in Nazi Germany* (Oxford: Oxford University Press, 1998), 142.

12. Ibid., 138.

13. Beate Meyer, Hermann Simon, and Chana Schütz, *Jews in Nazi Berlin: From Kristallnacht to Liberation* (Chicago: University of Chicago Press, 2009), 125.

14. Kaplan, *Between Dignity and Despair,* 139.

15. Ibid., 140.

16. This is not to suggest that women and children were never the targets of Nazi violence. During Kristallnacht, it was reported that women and children in Leipzig were driven into the shallow river, where they were forced to stand for hours in the cold water. In Karlsruhe, the children in the Jewish children's home were put into the street. Still, at this point, the primary victims of physical attacks were male.

17. Ruth Kluger, *Landscapes of Memory: A Holocaust Girlhood Remembered* (London: Bloomsbury, 2001), 30.

18. The HICEM was an international Jewish organization, established in 1927 to deal with Jewish migration. It was set up by three organizations: HIAS (the Hebrew Sheltering and Immigrant Aid Society, an American Jewish organization based in New York), ICA (Jewish Colonization Association, based in Great Britain), and Emig-Direkt (founded in Berlin in 1921). HICEM is an acronym for HIAS, ICA, and Emig-Direkt.

19. "The Situation in Shanghai," HICEM report, YIVO Archives, HICEM Collection, box 70, folder xvc-3.

20. Kaplan, *Between Dignity and Despair*, 143.

21. Ibid.

22. C. Wild, *Baden-Baden and the Black Forest* (1886), 4.

23. Alfons Isack Gestapo file, Landesarchiv Nordrhein-Westfalen, Düsseldorf.

24. Ibid.

25. According to his file, the suspension was based on Hitler's amnesty granted to the civilian population on September 9, 1939.

26. Kaplan, *Between Dignity and Despair*, 21.

12. Deportation to Gurs

1. "Reich Reported Deporting Jews to Poland, France," Jewish Telegraphic Agency, October 29, 1940, vol. 7, no. 170.

2. US State Department Records, 1940, LM 193, reel 58, National Archives.

3. Hilde Übelacker came back to Germany in 1946. She had escaped to Switzerland four years earlier with the assistance of Protestant clergy in France. In 1952, she moved back into her childhood home with her husband. The farm family she had worked for as a teenager were her "best friends as long as they lived."

4. Hilde Übelacker, personal interview, Baden-Baden, Germany, May 26, 2011.

5. Ibid. At this point the Nazis had not begun their policy of extermination. Death camps such as Auschwitz did not yet exist. But as early as October 1939, following the invasion of Poland, Jews had been uprooted and deported to inhospitable areas in the east. See Deborah E. Lipstadt, *The Eichmann Trial* (New York: Random House, 2011), 75.

6. Übelacker interview.

7. "Report on the Deportation of German Jews to Southern France," Karlsruhe in Baden-Württemberg, October 30, 1940, Politisches Archiv Auswärtiges Amt (PA/AA), R 100869, Berlin.

8. Ibid.

9. Ibid.

10. Achim Reimer, *Stadt zwischen zwei Demokratien: Baden-Baden von 1930 bis 1950* (Bern: Peter Lang, 2005), 130.

11. "Report on the Deportation of German Jews to Southern France."

12. "Verzeichnis der am 22. Oktober 1940 aus Baden ausgewiesenen Juden," Stadtmuseum/Stadtarchiv, Baden-Baden, 3–5.

13. Manfred Kirschner, personal interview, Pembrooke Pines, FL, July 2012.

14. *Trials of War Criminals Before the Nuernberg Tribunal Under Control Council Law No. 10*, vol. 13 (Washington, DC: US Government Printing Office, 1952), 165.

15. Angelika Schindler, personal interview, Baden-Baden, Germany, May 2012.

16. The Baden transport was originally conceived as a trial run. The Nazis hoped to deport 270,000 Jews from the Old Reich, Austria, and the Protectorate of Bohemia and Moravia to Vichy France. French opposition apparently derailed this plan. See Appendix, "Report on the Deportation of German Jews to Southern France."

17. Übelacker interview.

18. Ibid.

19. Susan Zuccotti, *The Holocaust, the French, and the Jews* (New York: Basic Books, 1993), 65.

20. Letter from Herbert Katzki, October 27, 1940, American Jewish Joint Distribution Committee (hereinafter AJDC) Archives, Collection 33/44, file 618, no. 2 of 2.

21. "Report on the Deportation of German Jews to Southern France."

22. "Refugees in French Concentration Camps," pamphlet, AJDC Archives, Collection 33/44, fol. 619, no. 2 of 2.

23. Hanne Hirsch Liebmann, interview, United States Holocaust Memorial Museum, 1990, available at: http://www.ushmm.org/wlc/en/media_oi.php?MediaId=1652.

24. Kirschner interview.

25. Quoted in Zuccotti, *Holocaust, French, and Jews*, 66.

26. If Arnold had not met the first two requirements for sending money to unoccupied France, he would have needed to file an application for permission to transmit funds with the US Treasury Department.

27. Letter from HICEM staffer to HIAS office, New York, December 6, 1940, AJDC Archives, Collection 33/44, folder 619, no. 1 of 2.

28. Letter by Joseph J. Schwartz, February 12, 1941, AJDC Archives, Collection 33/44, folder 619.

29. Zuccotti, *Holocaust, French, and Jews,* 67.

30. Michael Merose, Marta's grandson and Dora's great-nephew, shared this letter with the AJC Archives. It is his belief that the letter was probably his grandmother Marta's last letter, written shortly before her death in 1941. He is uncertain whether it was ever sent.

31. Report on internment camps, February 1941, AJDC Archives, Collection 33/44, folder 619, no. 1 of 2.

32. Ibid.

33. Übelacker interview.

34. Kirschner interview.

35. Oskar Wolf Diary, 1940–1941, Stadtmuseum/Stadtarchiv, Baden-Baden, 1.

36. Ibid., 22.

37. Letter from an aid worker, November 16, 1941, AJDC Archives, Collection 33/44, folder 620, no. 2 of 2.

38. Report prepared by Dr. J. W., translated January 30, 1941, AJDC Archives, Collection 33/44, folder 619, no. 1 of 2.

39. Übelacker interview.

40. Ellen Bonnell, American Friends Service Committee, Marseille, report for the Philadelphia office, January 7, 1941, AJDC Archives, Collection 33/44, fol. 619, no. 1 of 2.

41. Unitarian Service Committee Assistance Report, February 19, 1941, AJDC Archives, Collection 33/44, folder 619, no. 1 of 2.

42. Statement by Dr. Joseph H. Schwartz, May 5, 1941, AJDC Archives, Collection 33/44, folder 619, no. 2 of 2.

43. Those transferred out of Gurs in 1941, unless they had the good fortune of escaping or emigrating, had a short reprieve. In August 1942, the Nazis issued an order calling for the deportation of foreign Jews from unoccupied France to the east.

44. "Information Service Report No. #, The Camp de Gurs," January 15, 1941, AJDC Archives, Collection 33/44, folder 619, no. 1 of 2.

45. Unitarian Service Committee Assistance report.

13. A Closing Door

1. The Germans had surrendered in May 1945, but war did not end in the Pacific until the atomic bombings of Hiroshima on August 6 and Nagasaki on August 9, 1945.

Conclusion

1. Moise Moiseff, "Jewish Transits in Japan," HIAS Records, YIVO Archives, Record Group 245.4, XV, C7.

2. Their names are included in the list of Lodz ghetto inhabitants, 1940–1944, Yad Vashem Archives. This determination was also made by the Yad Vashem Archives due to information from the organization of former residents of Lodz in Israel, Jerusalem 1994.

3. Gerri Rozanski, personal interview, New York, February 2009.

4. Ibid.

5. Ibid.

6. "AJC Committee Veteran Awarded Germany's Order of Merit," AJC press release, New York, October 6, 1992.

7. "Remarks by Luzie Hatch on the Presentation to Her of the Order of Merit of the Federal Republic of Germany at the New York German Consulate General," September 24, 1992, Luzie Hatch Collection, American Jewish Committee Archives.

Appendix

1. The part of the Palatinate that was then part of Bavaria. It is located immediately east of the Saar.

INDEX

Index

—

288

Index
—

Index
—

Index

—

293